Secrets of the Bone Labyrinth: The Haunted Catacombs of Paris

Edward Turner

Published by Oliver Lancaster, 2023.

While every precaution has been taken in the preparation of this book, the publisher assumes no responsibility for errors or omissions, or for damages resulting from the use of the information contained herein.

SECRETS OF THE BONE LABYRINTH: THE HAUNTED CATACOMBS OF PARIS

First edition. August 4, 2023.

ISBN: 979-8223729341

Written by Edward Turner.

Also by Edward Turner

The Kraken Quest: Exploring the Mythical Giants of the Sea
Secrets of the Bone Labyrinth: The Haunted Catacombs of
Paris

Sign up to my free newsletter to get updates on new releases, FREE teaser chapters to upcoming releases and FREE digital short stories.

Or visit https://tinyurl.com/olanc

I never spam and you can unsubscribe at any time.

Disclaimer

The content presented in "Secrets of the Bone Labyrinth: The Haunted Catacombs of Paris" is based on historical records, eyewitness accounts, and credible research. While efforts have been made to ensure accuracy, the author and publisher are not liable for any inaccuracies, misinterpretations, or actions taken based on the information provided. Urban exploration of the Catacombs is illegal and dangerous, and readers are advised to respect all laws, safety measures, and historical preservation efforts.

———————————————

Secrets of the Bone Labyrinth: The Haunted Catacombs of Paris

SECRETS OF THE BONE LABYRINTH: THE HAUNTED CATACOMBS OF PARIS

Chapter 1: The Veiled History of Parisian Catacombs

───

The Catacombs of Paris, famously known as "The Bone Labyrinth," hold a sinister allure that has captivated the imaginations of visitors and storytellers alike. These macabre underground tunnels, filled with the skeletal remains of millions of Parisians, have a rich and intriguing history that dates back centuries.

The story of the Catacombs begins with the city's geology. Paris rests upon a vast underground network of limestone quarries that were actively mined since Roman times for the construction of buildings and monuments. The extraction of limestone continued through the medieval era and into the 18th century, leaving extensive tunnels and caverns beneath the city.

By the late 18th century, Paris faced a significant problem. The city's cemeteries were becoming overcrowded, posing a public health hazard. The cemeteries were not only running out of space, but the decaying bodies were contaminating the city's drinking water and air, leading to outbreaks of diseases.

In 1786, amid mounting public health concerns, the authorities made a critical decision to address this predicament. They ordered the closure of several cemeteries and began relocating the remains to the abandoned limestone quarries, creating a massive ossuary in the process.

The transformation of the quarries into an ossuary was a monumental task, requiring meticulous planning and execution. The endeavor commenced in 1786 and took several years to complete. The skeletal remains from various cemeteries across Paris were exhumed and carefully transferred to the Catacombs.

The relocation of the bones served both practical and symbolic purposes. The practical aspect involved resolving the issue of overcrowded cemeteries and mitigating the public health hazards they posed. The symbolic dimension, however, was equally significant. The transfer of the remains to the Catacombs was seen as a way to honor and commemorate the dead, creating a sacred space beneath the bustling city streets.

Engineers and laborers worked diligently to organize the bones, creating intricate patterns and designs with skulls and femurs, forming the haunting displays that visitors witness today. This arrangement was not only a testament to the skill and craftsmanship of the workers but also served as a somber reminder of the transient nature of human existence.

Throughout the 19th and 20th centuries, the Catacombs remained relatively unknown to the general public, accessible only to a select few. However, during the 19th century, the Catacombs started to gain popularity among curious explorers and adventurers who were drawn to the eerie underground realm.

In the early 19th century, the Catacombs experienced a period of romantic fascination, with artists, writers, and poets exploring the dark tunnels to seek inspiration for their works. They found the Catacombs to be a hauntingly beautiful place, and their accounts contributed to the mystique that still surrounds these underground passages.

During World War II, the Catacombs also played a role in the French Resistance, serving as a hiding place for resistance fighters and valuable cultural artifacts. The tunnels provided a strategic location for evasion and concealment from German occupiers.

In the contemporary era, the Catacombs have become a major tourist attraction in Paris, drawing thousands of visitors each year. However, access to the Catacombs is strictly regulated to preserve the delicate ossuary and ensure visitor safety. Only a small portion of the extensive underground network is open to the public.

The dark and mysterious nature of the Catacombs has inspired numerous haunting legends and ghostly tales over the years. These stories have been passed down through generations, adding to the allure of the Bone Labyrinth.

One of the most famous legends is that of the "Catacombs' Guardian." According to the legend, the spirit of a former quarry worker guards the Catacombs, ensuring that the remains are respected and undisturbed. It is said that those who show disrespect or disregard for the ossuary may face the wrath of this spectral guardian.

Other stories speak of eerie voices and unexplained noises emanating from the depths of the Catacombs. Visitors have reported hearing whispers and distant cries, leading some to believe that the spirits of the deceased still inhabit these subterranean chambers.

Another spine-chilling tale is that of the "Lost Tourists." It is said that the Catacombs have a way of disorienting explorers, causing them to lose their way and wander aimlessly through the dark tunnels. Some versions of the story suggest that those who become lost may never find their way back to the surface, becoming permanent residents of the Bone Labyrinth.

While these tales are undoubtedly products of folklore and urban legends, they add an extra layer of mystery and excitement to the already haunting atmosphere of the Catacombs.

Preserving the Catacombs and protecting its delicate contents have been ongoing priorities for the French authorities. The delicate balance between promoting tourism and safeguarding the historical site is a constant challenge.

To prevent overcrowding and potential damage to the ossuary, visitor numbers are carefully controlled, and guided tours are the only means of access. The Catacombs are also equipped with monitoring systems to detect any unusual activities and unauthorized entry.

Furthermore, the limestone structures within the Catacombs are susceptible to degradation due to the high humidity levels underground. To counteract this, conservationists work to maintain stable environmental conditions and conduct periodic restoration efforts to ensure the longevity of this unique historical monument.

The Secrets of the Bone Labyrinth, the Haunted Catacombs of Paris, represent a fascinating intersection of history, art, and mortality. From their humble origins as limestone quarries to their transformation into a sacred ossuary, the Catacombs have continued to captivate and intrigue generations of visitors.

The haunting beauty and chilling legends surrounding this subterranean realm stand as a testament to the human fascination with life, death, and the unknown. As one descends into the depths of the Catacombs, they embark on a journey through time, contemplating the impermanence of existence and the enduring legacy of those who came before us.

While the Catacombs continue to draw curious souls seeking to uncover the mysteries that lie within, it is crucial to remember the significance of preserving and respecting this unique historical site. As long as the Catacombs stand beneath the bustling streets of Paris, they will continue to be a symbol of remembrance and a poignant reminder of our mortality.

As a place of both historical significance and tourism interest, the Catacombs of Paris have been the subject of ethical dilemmas and controversies. Balancing the preservation of cultural heritage, respect for the deceased, and the demands of tourism presents complex challenges.

One of the primary ethical dilemmas is the question of whether the Catacombs should remain open to the public at all. Some argue that the sheer number of visitors can have a detrimental impact on the delicate ossuary, leading to the deterioration of bones and artifacts. Additionally, the influx of tourists may not always show the necessary respect for the site and the deceased, potentially desecrating this sacred space.

On the other hand, proponents of keeping the Catacombs accessible to the public believe that it serves an educational purpose. By allowing visitors to witness this unique historical monument, they can learn about the city's past, its geology, and the importance of respecting the dead. Controlled tourism also generates revenue, which can be used for conservation efforts and infrastructure improvements.

Conservationists and heritage experts play a crucial role in navigating these ethical challenges. They continuously monitor the Catacombs' condition, devise measures to maintain stability, and ensure that the site is not exploited for commercial purposes. Striking a balance between accessibility and preservation is an ongoing endeavor, with decisions subject to scrutiny and debate.

In light of the ethical concerns surrounding the Catacombs, responsible tourism practices are essential for preserving the site and honoring its historical and cultural significance. The authorities have implemented strict visitor guidelines to protect both visitors and the ossuary itself.

Tourists are required to be part of guided tours, ensuring that they follow designated paths and avoid venturing into restricted areas. These tours are also an opportunity to educate visitors about the history and significance of the Catacombs, promoting respect and awareness.

Photography is allowed within the Catacombs but must be done without flash to prevent damage to the bones and artifacts. Visitors are also advised to keep noise levels to a minimum, out of respect for the deceased and other visitors seeking a contemplative experience.

It is vital for visitors to understand that the Catacombs are not merely an attraction but a historical site with immense cultural value. Allowing time for reflection and contemplation while exploring the Bone Labyrinth can foster a more meaningful connection with the past and a deeper appreciation for the lives of those laid to rest within its walls.

Beyond tourism and conservation efforts, the Catacombs of Paris also attract the attention of scientific and historical researchers. These underground passages hold valuable information about the city's past, providing insights into various aspects of life and death during different periods.

Archaeologists and anthropologists study the bones and artifacts within the Catacombs to understand burial practices, disease patterns, and living conditions of past generations. These studies contribute to our knowledge of the history of Paris and its people, shedding light on aspects that might have been forgotten or overlooked in historical records.

The Catacombs also serve as an archive of the city's past, offering glimpses into the lives of ordinary people and notable figures alike. Researchers have made discoveries that link specific individuals buried in the Catacombs to notable events or historical periods, enriching our understanding of the past.

Furthermore, ongoing research helps in the conservation efforts by providing insights into the environmental conditions within the Catacombs. Understanding the impact of humidity, temperature, and other factors allows experts to implement measures to protect the site better.

Despite centuries of exploration and research, the Catacombs of Paris continue to harbor mysteries that remain unsolved. The vast underground network extends far beyond the area accessible to the public, leaving much of it uncharted and shrouded in darkness.

Urban legends and stories of hidden chambers, secret passageways, and lost treasures add to the mystique surrounding the Catacombs. These tales have spurred adventurers and explorers to embark on unauthorized journeys into the forbidden sections of the Bone Labyrinth, often with severe consequences.

However, venturing into the uncharted depths of the Catacombs is illegal and dangerous. Unauthorized explorers risk getting lost, encountering hazardous conditions, or facing legal repercussions. The authorities take such trespassing seriously and maintain efforts to deter unauthorized entry for the safety of both the explorers and the delicate ossuary.

Despite the mysteries that persist, the Catacombs of Paris continue to stand as a testament to the city's history and its resilience through the ages. The haunting beauty and solemn atmosphere of this underground necropolis leave an indelible impression on all who visit, inviting contemplation of life, death, and the enduring human spirit.

The Secrets of the Bone Labyrinth, the Haunted Catacombs of Paris, reveal a world beneath the bustling city streets that captivates the imagination and tugs at the heartstrings. From their humble origins as limestone quarries to their transformation into an ossuary and tourist attraction, the Catacombs have remained an enigmatic symbol of the cycle of life and death.

As visitors descend into the depths of the Bone Labyrinth, they embark on a journey through time, where history, art, and mystery converge. The haunting beauty of this subterranean realm, coupled with the eerie legends and ethical dilemmas it entails, leave an enduring mark on all who dare to explore its depths.

As we continue to unravel the enigmas of the Catacombs and seek to balance preservation with accessibility, let us remember the sacredness of this site and the stories it preserves. The Catacombs stand as a poignant reminder of our mortality and the collective memory of a city whose bones have become an eternal part of its labyrinthine heart. May we walk through its dimly lit passages with reverence, acknowledging the past while cherishing the present, as we navigate the Secrets of the Bone Labyrinth: The Haunted Catacombs of Paris.

EDWARD TURNER

Chapter 2: Descending into Darkness

———

The journey into the depths of the Catacombs of Paris begins with an eerie descent. As visitors leave the bustling streets behind and step into the unassuming entrance, a sense of foreboding anticipation creeps over them. A narrow spiral staircase leads downward into the dark abyss below, and as they descend, the sounds of the city above fade into an eerie silence.

The air becomes heavy with the musty scent of damp earth and the faint scent of limestone. Dimly lit lanterns sporadically placed along the walls cast flickering shadows, creating an atmosphere that feels both mystical and haunting. With every step deeper into the catacombs, the temperature drops, sending shivers down the spine.

Upon reaching the lower levels, visitors find themselves amid a seemingly endless labyrinth of bones. Skulls and femurs are meticulously arranged in neat rows and patterns, forming walls and arches that give the impression of an underground cathedral of death.

The silence is broken only by the echoes of whispered conversations among fellow visitors. The soft, reverent voices convey a shared understanding of the solemnity of the place. Everyone treads lightly, as if walking on hallowed ground, mindful of the remains surrounding them.

The dim lighting casts eerie shadows on the hollow eye sockets of the skulls, creating an illusion of movement. Some visitors claim to have seen spectral figures lurking in the dark corners, their existence questioned by the flickering light, while others speak of feeling an inexplicable presence, as if the spirits of the deceased are still lingering within the Bone Labyrinth.

As visitors venture deeper into the catacombs, the darkness intensifies. Guided tours may provide a sense of security, but the vastness of the unexplored areas looms in the imagination. Many passages remain off-limits, adding an air of mystery to the journey.

The uneven stone floors and narrow passages force visitors to bend and twist through tight spaces. The confined nature of the tunnels contributes to the sensation of being swallowed by the very earth itself. The catacombs seem to stretch infinitely, with no end in sight, giving rise to feelings of claustrophobia and vulnerability.

The air becomes chillier, and a damp mist clings to the walls, as if the catacombs are exhaling the breath of the deceased. Whispers of cold air brush against visitors' necks, prompting them to look over their shoulders, half-expecting to catch a glimpse of something ethereal.

Guides share tales of haunting legends that surround the Catacombs, adding to the eerie atmosphere. The story of the "Catacombs' Guardian" resurfaces, and visitors may find themselves glancing over their shoulders, half-expecting to catch a glimpse of the spectral figure.

SECRETS OF THE BONE LABYRINTH: THE HAUNTED CATACOMBS OF PARIS

The legend of the "Lost Tourists" also weighs on the minds of those who tread the catacombs' shadowy passages. Thoughts of becoming disoriented and separated from the group, forever lost in the dark labyrinth, send shivers down spines.

Some visitors recall accounts of mysterious sounds, whispers, and distant cries that seem to emanate from nowhere, heightening the sense of an unseen presence lurking within the darkness.

After what feels like an eternity of wandering through the depths of the Catacombs, the journey eventually reaches its conclusion. As visitors ascend the narrow staircase and emerge back into the world above, they find themselves blinking in the sudden brightness of daylight.

The contrast between the ethereal world below and the vibrant life above is stark. They breathe a sigh of relief, grateful to have escaped the chilling embrace of the Bone Labyrinth. However, an indescribable sense of awe and respect lingers, leaving an enduring impression on their souls.

As they leave the Catacombs behind, visitors can't help but reflect on the experience. The eerie journey into the depths of the Catacombs has not only taken them through the history of Paris and the lives of the deceased but has also invited contemplation of their own mortality. The haunting beauty and solemn atmosphere of the underground necropolis will forever be etched in their memories, and the mysteries that lie within will continue to beckon curious souls to delve into the Secrets of the Bone Labyrinth.

The eerie journey into the depths of the Catacombs leaves an indelible impression on the minds of those who experience it. Visitors find themselves haunted by the images of the meticulously arranged bones, the haunting echoes of whispered conversations, and the chilling shadows that seemed to dance on the walls.

The sense of reverence and solemnity cultivated during the expedition lingers long after returning to the world above. The catacombs serve as a reminder of the impermanence of life, the interconnectedness of humanity, and the inevitability of mortality.

For some, the experience becomes a catalyst for introspection, prompting contemplation of life's purpose, the passage of time, and the legacies we leave behind. The Bone Labyrinth acts as a somber teacher, reminding us to cherish the present and reflect on the transience of life.

Throughout history, the Catacombs of Paris have inspired artists, writers, and poets alike. The eerie beauty of the subterranean realm has served as a muse, sparking creative expressions that explore themes of life, death, and the unknown.

Renowned authors such as Victor Hugo and Edgar Allan Poe have incorporated elements of the Catacombs into their literary works, infusing their stories with the haunting ambiance of the Bone Labyrinth. Painters have sought to capture the ethereal essence of the catacombs' architecture, creating haunting and surreal masterpieces that stand as testament to the enduring fascination with this subterranean realm.

The Catacombs' unique appeal lies not only in its macabre setting but also in the emotions and introspection it evokes. Artists find themselves drawn to the duality of the site—the stark reminder of mortality juxtaposed with the serene beauty of the carefully arranged bones.

As the Bone Labyrinth continues to captivate the imagination of visitors from all walks of life, its legacy endures as a symbol of Parisian history and the human condition. The Catacombs of Paris have become a cherished part of the city's cultural heritage, cherished for its unique historical significance and its ability to inspire contemplation and reflection.

In the modern era, the Catacombs stand as a testimony to the importance of responsible tourism and conservation. The delicate balance between accessibility and preservation remains a continuous challenge, as authorities strive to protect this sacred site while allowing visitors to glimpse into the city's past.

The Bone Labyrinth serves as a poignant reminder that the past is not confined to dusty history books but lives beneath the streets, woven into the very fabric of the city. It is a place where the tales of millions rest eternally, and where visitors find themselves drawn to confront the mysteries of life, death, and the human spirit.

The eerie journey into the depths of the Catacombs of Paris is a transformative experience that transcends time and space. It is a voyage that takes visitors through the layers of history, into the heart of the city's past and the essence of the human experience.

As visitors emerge from the haunting darkness of the Bone Labyrinth and return to the world of the living, they carry with them a newfound appreciation for life and an acknowledgment of the transient nature of existence.

The Secrets of the Bone Labyrinth, the Haunted Catacombs of Paris, continue to beckon curious souls, inviting them to explore the mysteries that lie beneath the city's surface. The Catacombs remain a testament to the enduring fascination with life, death, and the enigmatic stories of those who have passed through the Bone Labyrinth before us.

As the echoes of the past continue to resonate within these haunting passages, the Catacombs of Paris will forever be a symbol of remembrance, a place where the human spirit finds solace and inspiration, and a timeless reminder of the intricate dance between life and death that defines the human experience.

To ensure the safety and preservation of the Catacombs of Paris, access to the underground maze is strictly regulated. Visitors are not allowed to explore the Catacombs on their own. Instead, guided tours are the only means of experiencing this haunting underground realm.

Licensed tour operators, approved by the authorities, conduct these tours. Each group is limited in size to prevent overcrowding and to maintain a controlled environment. Tour guides are well-versed in the history of the Catacombs, the legends surrounding the site, and the safety protocols necessary for a smooth and secure visit.

Entrance to the Catacombs is restricted to specific access points, and unauthorized entry is strictly prohibited. This measure ensures that visitors do not get lost in the vast network of tunnels and passages beyond the designated tour routes.

At the entry points, security personnel check tickets and ensure that visitors are part of an authorized guided tour. This process also helps to monitor the number of people inside the Catacombs at any given time, preventing overcrowding and potential safety hazards.

The Catacombs are dimly lit, creating an eerie ambiance that adds to the mystique of the experience. However, the lighting is carefully designed to provide adequate visibility for visitors to navigate safely through the passages and observe the bone arrangements.

Lanterns or strategically placed electric lights illuminate the tour paths, ensuring that visitors can see where they are walking while also preserving the haunting atmosphere. The pathways are maintained and kept clear of debris to avoid tripping hazards and accidents.

To address potential emergencies, the Catacombs are equipped with emergency exits strategically placed throughout the underground complex. These exits are clearly marked and accessible in case of any unforeseen situations, such as a power outage or evacuation needs.

Furthermore, communication systems are in place to maintain contact between the tour guides and the surface personnel. This enables immediate response to any emergency situations that may arise during the tours.

The Catacombs are equipped with monitoring systems to detect any unusual activities, trespassers, or security breaches. Surveillance cameras and motion sensors are in place to ensure the safety of both visitors and the historical site.

Security personnel actively monitor the surveillance feeds from a central control room, providing an added layer of protection for this unique historical monument.

Before the tours begin, visitors are briefed on safety guidelines and rules that must be followed during the expedition. These guidelines cover essential aspects such as:

- Staying with the group and not wandering off alone.

- Avoiding touching the bones or any artifacts within the Catacombs.

- Keeping noise levels to a minimum, out of respect for the deceased and other visitors seeking a contemplative experience.

- Not using flash photography to prevent damage to the bones and artifacts.

- Being mindful of the low ceilings and uneven terrain to avoid accidents.

SECRETS OF THE BONE LABYRINTH: THE HAUNTED CATACOMBS OF PARIS

- Not smoking or bringing any flammable items into the Catacombs due to the fire hazard posed by the wooden structures.

Preserving the delicate ossuary and maintaining a safe environment is an ongoing endeavor. Conservationists continuously monitor the environmental conditions within the Catacombs to prevent degradation of the limestone structures and to protect the bones and artifacts.

Efforts to stabilize humidity levels, prevent water seepage, and mitigate the impact of visitors on the site's integrity are vital components of the conservation work.

Visiting the haunting underground maze of the Catacombs of Paris requires strict adherence to safety measures and guidelines. Regulated access, guided tours, controlled entry points, lighting, emergency exits, monitoring, and visitor safety guidelines all play crucial roles in ensuring the well-being of both visitors and the historical site.

As visitors descend into the depths of the Bone Labyrinth, they are immersed in a unique experience that fosters contemplation, reverence, and a deep appreciation for history and life. The careful balance between accessibility and preservation serves to protect this sacred underground realm, preserving its allure and mystery for generations to come.

Before embarking on the eerie journey into the depths of the Catacombs, visitors must prepare themselves physically and mentally for the experience. The Bone Labyrinth demands a level of respect and understanding due to its historical and cultural significance.

Tour operators provide essential information to visitors before the tours begin. They emphasize the importance of following the safety guidelines and respecting the solemnity of the site. Visitors are encouraged to dress appropriately, wearing comfortable shoes suitable for walking on uneven surfaces and in cool temperatures.

Additionally, visitors are advised to bring water and a small snack, as the tours may take several hours to complete. The underground environment can be deceptively draining, and staying hydrated is essential.

As visitors descend into the Catacombs, a mix of emotions floods their senses. The haunting beauty and chilling atmosphere create an ambiance like no other. The echoes of history reverberate through the tunnels, fostering a deep sense of connection with the past.

Tour guides lead visitors through the designated pathways, pointing out historical landmarks and explaining the significance of the bone arrangements. They share stories and legends that have been passed down through generations, adding to the intrigue and fascination of the experience.

Throughout the tour, visitors are encouraged to reflect on the lives of those interred within the Catacombs and the impact of their presence on the world above. The catacombs act as a poignant reminder of the interconnectedness of all humanity, transcending time and societal boundaries.

SECRETS OF THE BONE LABYRINTH: THE HAUNTED CATACOMBS OF PARIS

Despite the haunting allure of the Catacombs, safety remains the top priority. Visitors must stay vigilant and adhere to the instructions provided by the tour guides. The designated pathways are carefully maintained, but it is crucial to watch one's step and avoid touching any of the historical artifacts.

The underground environment can be challenging for those with certain medical conditions, such as claustrophobia or respiratory issues. If visitors have any concerns about their ability to handle the conditions in the Catacombs, they should consult with their tour operator beforehand.

The importance of staying with the guided group cannot be overstated. The Catacombs are an intricate maze, and venturing off alone can lead to getting lost or injured. Being aware of one's surroundings and staying close to the guide is essential for a safe and fulfilling experience.

Responsible tourism also means leaving no trace behind. Visitors are reminded to be mindful of the environment and not to disturb any bones or artifacts within the Catacombs. Graffiti, littering, or any actions that could cause harm to the site or disrespect the deceased are strictly forbidden.

Guided tours emphasize the significance of preserving the Bone Labyrinth for future generations. Each visitor plays a part in safeguarding this unique historical monument and ensuring that it remains a place of reflection and reverence for years to come.

As visitors emerge from the haunting depths of the Catacombs, they find themselves forever changed by the experience. The eerie journey leaves an enduring mark on their hearts and minds, fostering a deeper appreciation for history, mortality, and the interconnectedness of all life.

The Catacombs of Paris stand as a testament to the city's past and the resilience of the human spirit. As visitors return to the vibrant streets above, they carry with them the echoes of the Bone Labyrinth, forever haunted by the Catacombs of Paris.

Visiting the haunting underground maze of the Catacombs of Paris is a profound and transformative experience. From the meticulous safety measures and controlled access to the guided tours and visitor guidelines, the Bone Labyrinth demands a level of respect and responsibility.

The journey into the Catacombs leaves visitors in awe of the haunting beauty, immersed in history, and reminded of the fragility of life. The experience fosters a deep sense of connection with the past and an appreciation for the present. As visitors leave the Bone Labyrinth, they carry with them a newfound reverence for the deceased and an enduring mark left by the Secrets of the Bone Labyrinth: The Haunted Catacombs of Paris.

SECRETS OF THE BONE LABYRINTH: THE HAUNTED CATACOMBS OF PARIS

Chapter 3: The Subterranean Architecture

―――――

The Catacombs of Paris are not only a haunting ossuary but also an architectural marvel. The vast network of underground tunnels stretches over 300 kilometers (186 miles), forming an intricate labyrinth beneath the streets of the French capital.

The architecture of the Catacombs dates back centuries, with the earliest sections being the result of limestone quarrying. The quarries were carefully excavated to extract the valuable building material used in constructing Parisian monuments such as Notre-Dame Cathedral and the Louvre Museum.

The engineering ingenuity of the Catacombs lies in the construction of the quarry tunnels and their characteristic vaulted ceilings. Quarrying the limestone required meticulous planning and precise cutting techniques to ensure stability and prevent cave-ins.

The ceilings of the tunnels are a testament to the architectural prowess of the quarry workers. The vaulted design allowed for better distribution of the weight of the earth above, minimizing the risk of collapses and creating spacious passageways.

As the quarry tunnels were transformed into an ossuary, additional engineering efforts were undertaken to reinforce and stabilize the structures. Over time, as the catacombs expanded, certain sections required additional support to prevent subsidence.

Wooden beams and supports were strategically placed to shore up the walls and ceilings of the catacombs, ensuring their longevity and safety. These engineering feats have enabled the catacombs to withstand the test of time, preserving the city's history beneath its bustling surface.

The arrangement of bones within the Catacombs demonstrates both artistic talent and engineering precision. The skulls and femurs are carefully stacked in decorative patterns, creating hauntingly beautiful displays.

Skulls are often arranged to form heart shapes, crosses, and other intricate designs. The femurs are stacked horizontally to form walls and archways, creating an otherworldly ambiance that leaves visitors in awe of the craftsmanship.

The catacombs' underground nature necessitated engineering solutions for ventilation and lighting. Throughout the tunnels, ventilation shafts were strategically placed to allow air to circulate and prevent stagnation.

Lighting was originally provided by oil lamps, but as technology advanced, electric lighting was introduced. The eerie glow of lanterns and electric lights creates a haunting atmosphere that contributes to the mystique of the catacombs.

Managing water within the Catacombs was another engineering challenge. The catacombs lie beneath the water table, making them susceptible to flooding. To combat this, engineers implemented drainage systems and channels to divert water away from the passageways.

These water management techniques have played a crucial role in maintaining the stability of the catacombs and preserving the historical artifacts within.

In the modern era, the focus of engineering within the Catacombs has shifted towards conservation. As the catacombs continue to draw thousands of visitors each year, preserving the structures and artifacts becomes paramount.

Engineering experts work tirelessly to monitor the environmental conditions within the catacombs, ensuring that humidity, temperature, and other factors are carefully regulated to prevent degradation of the limestone structures and bones.

The architectural wonders and engineering feats of the Catacombs of Paris continue to fascinate visitors and researchers alike. This underground city of stone stands as a timeless legacy, a testament to human ingenuity, and a poignant reminder of the impermanence of life.

As visitors descend into the depths of the catacombs, they bear witness to the remarkable craftsmanship of past generations. The engineering marvels that lie beneath the streets of Paris illuminate not only the city's history but also the ability of humanity to create enduring structures that transcend time and continue to captivate the world centuries later. The Catacombs of Paris remain an everlasting wonder, revealing their haunting secrets to those willing to explore the architectural wonders and engineering feats of the Bone Labyrinth.

As visitors explore the architectural wonders of the Catacombs, they are also stepping into the annals of history. The underground labyrinth, with its carefully constructed tunnels and artistic bone arrangements, weaves a tapestry of stories from different eras.

Each section of the catacombs holds its own history, reflecting the different periods when quarrying, ossuary creation, and expansions took place. The catacombs stand as silent witnesses to the evolution of Paris, its growth, and its response to the challenges of burial and public health.

While guided tours offer a glimpse into the architectural marvels of the Catacombs, a significant portion of this underground realm remains unexplored by the public. The unseen sections are a testament to the immensity of the catacombs, hiding secrets and mysteries yet to be unveiled.

These uncharted areas fuel the imagination of adventurers and urban explorers, sparking legends and tales of hidden chambers and unknown passages. Despite the allure, unauthorized exploration is strictly forbidden, as the unexplored sections pose significant safety risks.

In recent decades, preservation efforts have become a focal point of the architectural wonders of the Catacombs. Conservationists and engineers work tirelessly to safeguard the structural integrity of the catacombs, ensuring that future generations can continue to experience this unique underground masterpiece.

Various methods, such as the use of specialized materials to reinforce weakened sections, are employed to maintain the catacombs' stability. In this delicate balance between preservation and accessibility, the aim is to conserve the catacombs' haunting beauty while allowing visitors to explore its mesmerizing depths safely.

The Catacombs of Paris stand not only as a burial site but also as an architectural wonder and a monument to the city's past. This underground world pays homage to the lives of the countless Parisians whose remains rest within its walls and serves as a tangible link to centuries of history.

The careful engineering and artistic bone arrangements reflect the respect and reverence for the deceased that motivated the creation of this unique ossuary. The catacombs transcend time, offering a glimpse into the lives, beliefs, and ingenuity of those who came before.

The architectural wonders and engineering feats of the Catacombs of Paris will continue to captivate visitors for generations to come. As the world above evolves, the catacombs remain a constant, timeless monument to the human spirit and the enduring significance of life and death.

For those who dare to descend into the depths of the Bone Labyrinth, the haunting beauty and history embedded within the catacombs will leave an everlasting mark on their souls. The catacombs stand as a reminder that beneath the bustling streets of Paris lies a realm of marvels and mysteries, where the past converges with the present, and where the Secrets of the Bone Labyrinth continue to beckon curious souls.

The construction of the Catacombs of Paris began in the late 18th century, but its origins can be traced back to the Middle Ages. As Paris grew, so did the need for construction materials, especially limestone, which was ideal for building sturdy structures.

The quarrying of limestone in the region of Paris started in the 13th century. As the demand for this valuable building material increased, the quarries expanded into an extensive underground network beneath the city. These quarry tunnels became known as the Catacombs.

Quarrying in the Catacombs was a labor-intensive process that required skilled workers. Miners would excavate the limestone using tools such as pickaxes, chisels, and saws. They would carefully extract large blocks of limestone from the walls of the tunnels.

The mined limestone was then transported to the surface using various means, including wooden carts and pulley systems. The removal of the limestone left behind large voids and galleries underground, creating the foundations for the Bone Labyrinth that would come to be.

The transformation of the quarry tunnels into an ossuary was prompted by the need to address public health concerns in the overcrowded cemeteries of Paris. By the end of the 18th century, the city's cemeteries were overflowing, leading to the risk of disease outbreaks.

To mitigate these issues, it was decided to relocate the remains of the deceased to the abandoned quarry tunnels. Between 1786 and 1788, the remains of millions of Parisians were transferred to the Catacombs, beginning the process of transforming the underground quarry into a city of the dead.

The underground layout of the Catacombs is intricate and labyrinthine, comprising a vast network of tunnels, galleries, and chambers. The tunnels extend over an area of more than 300 kilometers (186 miles), with varying levels of depth.

The layout is organized into different sections, each corresponding to specific periods of quarrying and ossuary creation. The galleries and pathways are carefully planned, with vaulted ceilings and stable structures that ensure the catacombs' long-term stability.

The public access area of the Catacombs is where guided tours take place and is open to visitors. This section features well-maintained pathways with artistic bone arrangements lining the walls.

The ossuary displays are thoughtfully arranged, with skulls and femurs forming patterns and designs that create an otherworldly ambiance. Throughout the public access area, information boards provide historical context, explaining the significance of the catacombs and its role in Parisian history.

Beyond the public access area lies the restricted and unexplored sections of the Catacombs. These areas are inaccessible to the general public and are off-limits due to safety concerns and the need to preserve the catacombs' integrity.

The restricted sections are essential for maintaining the catacombs' stability and preventing unauthorized access. The unexplored sections hold the allure of mystery, sparking legends and stories of hidden chambers and forgotten passages. However, venturing into these areas is strictly forbidden and poses significant dangers to those who attempt it.

The construction and layout of the underground tunnels of the Catacombs of Paris stand as a remarkable testament to human ingenuity and the value of adapting existing structures to serve new purposes. The careful planning, the engineering feats of the vaulted ceilings, and the artistic arrangements of bones all reflect the reverence for the deceased and the desire to create a lasting memorial.

The Catacombs not only serve as a haunting ossuary but also as an architectural marvel that weaves together the history of Paris, from its origins as a limestone quarry to its transformation into a city of the dead. This underground realm captures the essence of the city's past, immersing visitors in a journey through time and offering a poignant reminder of the cyclical nature of life and death.

As visitors explore the underground tunnels of the Catacombs, they bear witness to the craftsmanship and vision of generations past, leaving them in awe of the Catacombs of Paris.

Preserving the construction and layout of the underground tunnels presents a constant challenge for authorities and conservationists. The Catacombs, with their delicate limestone structures and historical artifacts, are susceptible to natural decay and the impact of human activity.

One of the primary concerns is maintaining the structural stability of the catacombs. Over time, the limestone walls and ceilings can deteriorate due to humidity, water infiltration, and other environmental factors. Conservation efforts involve monitoring the conditions within the catacombs to prevent further degradation and employing measures to reinforce weakened sections.

Environmental factors, such as temperature and humidity, play a significant role in the preservation of the catacombs. The underground environment is naturally cool, but humidity levels need to be carefully regulated to prevent the growth of mold and other forms of decay.

To address this, conservationists install dehumidifiers and employ ventilation systems to control the airflow within the catacombs. By carefully monitoring and adjusting these factors, the catacombs can be preserved for future generations to experience.

With thousands of visitors exploring the catacombs each year, managing the impact of tourism on the delicate structures is crucial. The public access area is designed to accommodate guided tours while protecting the bone arrangements and historical artifacts.

Visitor safety guidelines are strictly enforced to prevent accidental damage to the catacombs. Flash photography is prohibited to prevent discoloration and degradation of the bones, and visitors are instructed not to touch any of the historical structures or exhibits.

The artistic bone arrangements within the Catacombs require special care to preserve their integrity. Over time, dust and other particles can accumulate on the bones, affecting their appearance. Conservationists use specialized cleaning techniques to gently remove debris without causing damage.

Additionally, periodic assessments are conducted to monitor the condition of the bone arrangements. If any sections show signs of deterioration, experts intervene to repair and restore the artistic displays.

Finding the delicate balance between allowing public access to the catacombs and preserving their historical significance is a continuous challenge. The Catacombs of Paris hold immense cultural and educational value, making it essential to allow visitors to experience this unique site.

However, ensuring the safety and preservation of the catacombs is equally important. The strict regulation of access, guided tours, and restricted areas contribute to managing the delicate balance between accessibility and preservation.

SECRETS OF THE BONE LABYRINTH: THE HAUNTED CATACOMBS OF PARIS

The Catacombs of Paris remain an enduring legacy, a testament to human craftsmanship and adaptability. The construction and layout of the underground tunnels reflect the resourcefulness of past generations in transforming quarries into a profound and haunting memorial.

Preserving this unique architectural wonder requires the dedicated efforts of conservationists, engineers, and authorities. As technology and conservation practices continue to advance, the catacombs' legacy will endure, inviting future generations to delve into the mysteries of the Bone Labyrinth and contemplate the Secrets of the Haunted Catacombs of Paris.

EDWARD TURNER

Chapter 4: The Silent Guardians

———

Deep within the haunting depths of the Catacombs of Paris, an enigmatic presence lurks - the Cataflics. Shrouded in mystery, these guardians are a secretive group entrusted with the task of patrolling the underground labyrinth to deter trespassers and protect the historical site from unauthorized exploration.

The Cataflics' origins are steeped in folklore and legend, making it challenging to trace their exact history. Some accounts suggest that they were established in the 19th century when the Catacombs first opened to the public. Others claim that the Cataflics date back to much earlier periods when the catacombs were still a hidden realm, accessible only to a select few.

These guardians were initially tasked with ensuring the safety of visitors during tours and maintaining order within the Catacombs. However, as tales of uninvited adventurers and urban explorers grew, the Cataflics' responsibilities expanded to include deterring trespassers and preserving the catacombs' sanctity.

Operating under the cover of darkness, the Cataflics venture into the unexplored and restricted sections of the Catacombs. Equipped with lanterns and modern technology, they navigate the labyrinthine passages, ever watchful for signs of intruders.

Their identities are kept confidential, and their appearances are concealed behind dark robes and masks, adding to the mystique that surrounds them. The Cataflics are known to communicate through a series of gestures and signals, ensuring seamless coordination during their nocturnal patrols.

For the Cataflics, the protection of the Catacombs is more than a duty; it is a sacred calling. They view themselves as guardians of the memories and the deceased who rest in this underground necropolis.

The Cataflics take their role seriously, approaching their mission with a blend of reverence and solemnity. They believe that the catacombs hold a delicate balance between the living and the dead, and their presence is an essential aspect of maintaining this equilibrium.

In the subterranean world of the Catacombs, the Cataflics engage in a never-ending cat and mouse game with trespassers and urban explorers. While the Cataflics possess extensive knowledge of the tunnels and passages, the intruders often try to outwit and elude them.

Despite the challengers they face, the Cataflics remain persistent in their pursuit of deterring unauthorized access. They are familiar with the various entry points and routes used by trespassers and work diligently to secure these access points and reinforce them to prevent further unauthorized entries.

The Cataflics are not mere enforcers; they also act as guardians of wisdom and warnings. Upon encountering trespassers, they deliver a stern but subtle message of the catacombs' sanctity and the importance of respecting the final resting place of the deceased.

The guardians communicate through actions rather than words, ensuring that the trespassers understand the significance of their actions. For those who heed the warning and respect the sanctity of the catacombs, the Cataflics become ethereal figures, fading into the darkness as quickly as they appeared.

As the Cataflics continue their tireless vigil, their legacy of protection becomes deeply ingrained in the catacombs' lore. Their presence ensures that the catacombs remain a place of reverence and historical significance, guarded against those who seek to exploit or damage this sacred site.

While their identities may remain a secret and their work shrouded in mystery, the Cataflics' impact on the preservation of the Catacombs of Paris is undeniable. Their dedication to safeguarding this underground marvel ensures that the haunting secrets and architectural wonders of the Bone Labyrinth endure for generations to come. As the enigmatic guardians of the Catacombs, the Cataflics continue to play an essential role in maintaining the Secrets of the Haunted Catacombs of Paris.

The Cataflics operate under a code of silence, forming a closely-knit brotherhood dedicated to their mission. This silence not only helps maintain the aura of mystery surrounding them but also serves a practical purpose in their work.

The Cataflics communicate with each other using a combination of hand signals, gestures, and unspoken understanding. This unique form of communication allows them to coordinate seamlessly during their patrols without the need for verbal exchanges that might echo through the tunnels and draw unwanted attention.

Beyond their role in deterring trespassers, the Cataflics take pride in being protectors of Parisian history. They see themselves as the custodians of the city's past, ensuring that the Catacombs remain an authentic representation of the intricate relationship between life, death, and human ingenuity.

The Cataflics are well-versed in the historical significance of the catacombs, possessing a deep knowledge of the different sections, architectural wonders, and legends associated with the site. This knowledge is passed down from one generation of guardians to the next, preserving the continuity of their sacred duty.

While the world above rests in slumber, the Cataflics take on their nocturnal watch. The night becomes their ally, providing cover as they move through the catacombs, their lanterns casting eerie shadows along the limestone walls.

The Cataflics' ability to navigate the dark passages with precision and vigilance adds to their mystique. To some, they become mythical figures, part of the haunting tapestry of the catacombs' legends.

Over the years, a handful of adventurers and urban explorers have encountered the Cataflics during their illegal expeditions into the Catacombs. These encounters are shrouded in secrecy, and those who have faced the guardians often speak of an unsettling aura surrounding the figures in the dark robes.

Some trespassers claim to have been gently guided back to the exit by the Cataflics, while others describe feeling an overwhelming sense of respect for the site's history and the importance of preserving its sanctity.

As the Cataflics continue their eternal watch over the Catacombs, their legacy becomes deeply interwoven with the site's history. Their silent presence serves as a constant reminder that the Bone Labyrinth is not merely a tourist attraction but a place of deep significance.

Their dedication to their sacred duty, guarding the catacombs from those who would trespass and desecrate, ensures that the secrets and stories of the past continue to echo through the subterranean passages.

The Cataflics' legacy is a haunting one, reflecting their commitment to preserving the sanctity of the Catacombs of Paris. As the guardians of this underground realm, they protect the delicate balance between the living and the dead, ensuring that the memories of the past remain undisturbed.

Their identity hidden behind masks and robes, the Cataflics continue their silent watch, reminding visitors and trespassers alike of the haunting secrets that lie within the Bone Labyrinth.

For generations to come, the Cataflics will remain a symbol of the enduring devotion to preserving the historical significance and architectural wonders of the Catacombs of Paris. Their presence adds an air of enigma and reverence to this underground necropolis, perpetuating the Secrets of the Haunted Catacombs of Paris and the guardians who watch over them.

The Cataflics' task of protecting the subterranean realm is not without its challenges. Their primary adversary is the unseen enemy - trespassers who venture into the catacombs without permission. These intruders often arrive under the cover of darkness, seeking the thrill of exploring the forbidden underground world.

Despite the Cataflics' best efforts to secure access points, determined trespassers may find new entryways, forcing the guardians to constantly adapt their strategies to counter this relentless challenge.

The Catacombs of Paris comprise a vast and complex labyrinth of tunnels, galleries, and chambers. Navigating this intricate underground network presents an ongoing challenge for the Cataflics.

With over 300 kilometers (186 miles) of passageways to monitor, the guardians must remain vigilant to cover all areas effectively. The sheer size of the catacombs makes it challenging to ensure that every corner is safeguarded against trespassers.

Trespassers often catch the Cataflics off guard with their unexpected appearances. The vastness of the catacombs allows intruders to explore without being detected until they are deep within the underground realm.

SECRETS OF THE BONE LABYRINTH: THE HAUNTED CATACOMBS OF PARIS

The element of surprise can compromise the guardians' ability to respond swiftly, making it crucial for the Cataflics to rely on their keen senses and training to maintain a watchful eye on the catacombs at all times.

The Cataflics operate with limited resources, relying on their dedication and passion for the catacombs' protection. As a secretive and underground organization, they receive minimal support from official authorities, which can limit their ability to invest in advanced technology or personnel.

Despite these constraints, the Cataflics are resourceful, making the most of what they have to continue their sacred duty of safeguarding the subterranean realm.

The Cataflics must contend with the inherent dangers of the underground environment while conducting their patrols. Uneven terrain, low ceilings, and unstable limestone structures pose potential hazards to the guardians as they navigate the catacombs' passageways.

To mitigate risks, the Cataflics receive specialized training in underground safety and cave rescue techniques. However, the catacombs remain an inherently hazardous environment, and the guardians must always be prepared for unforeseen challenges.

Operating in secrecy, the Cataflics face legal constraints in dealing with trespassers. While they work to deter unauthorized access, they must adhere to the laws and regulations governing the catacombs and the urban environment.

This legal limitation can be frustrating for the Cataflics, as it may prevent them from taking more assertive action against trespassers. Instead, they often rely on warnings and symbolic gestures to communicate their message and protect the catacombs' sanctity.

A delicate balance exists between preserving the catacombs and actively protecting them from intruders. The Cataflics must consider the potential impact of their own actions on the delicate limestone structures and historical artifacts within the catacombs.

Preserving the site's integrity while deterring trespassers can be a complex challenge. The guardians strive to protect the catacombs from both external threats and any inadvertent harm that their own presence might cause.

The Cataflics operate in relative isolation, limiting their ability to call for immediate backup in case of emergencies. While this isolation allows them to maintain secrecy, it can also be a double-edged sword when facing unexpected or challenging situations.

The guardians rely on their training and communication skills to manage potential emergencies independently and make crucial decisions in the depths of the catacombs.

The responsibility of protecting the catacombs and ensuring the sanctity of the underground realm can take an emotional toll on the Cataflics. The constant vigilance, isolation, and encounters with trespassers can weigh heavily on their psyche.

SECRETS OF THE BONE LABYRINTH: THE HAUNTED CATACOMBS OF PARIS

However, their passion for the catacombs and their commitment to preserving this unique historical site keep the Cataflics dedicated to their sacred duty, providing them with a sense of purpose and fulfillment despite the challenges they face.

Despite the challenges they encounter, the Cataflics remain steadfast in their mission to protect the subterranean realm. They understand that their role as guardians is part of an enduring legacy, passed down through generations, and they strive to ensure that the catacombs' secrets and architectural wonders endure for future generations to discover and appreciate.

The Cataflics' commitment to preserving the Secrets of the Haunted Catacombs of Paris represents a timeless and solemn duty, an unwavering dedication to protecting the catacombs' sanctity and the memories of those who rest within the Bone Labyrinth.

As the Cataflics patrol the Catacombs of Paris, they often find themselves enveloped in an eerie and ghostly ambiance. The underground passages, shrouded in darkness, echo with the whispers of history and the memories of the deceased.

Navigating through the shadows, the guardians encounter haunting echoes of the past - spectral remnants of the countless souls laid to rest within the catacombs. The ghostly presence adds an ethereal layer to their duties, reminding them of the spiritual significance of their mission.

Guarding the Catacombs of Paris is not merely a physical endeavor; it also takes a toll on the Cataflics' psychological well-being. The constant exposure to the subterranean realm and its haunting atmosphere can leave a lasting impact on their minds.

The guardians often confront their own mortality and contemplate the mysteries of life and death as they navigate the catacombs. The isolation, darkness, and proximity to the deceased present unique psychological challenges, which the Cataflics must confront and process.

Despite the challenges they face, the Cataflics view their role as a test of their resolve and commitment to the catacombs' protection. They draw strength from their shared purpose and dedication to preserving this unique historical site.

In times of doubt or weariness, the Cataflics remind themselves of the importance of their sacred duty. Their collective determination fuels their unwavering vigilance, enabling them to continue their watch over the Bone Labyrinth.

The Cataflics form a unique and unbreakable bond with each other and the catacombs they protect. Their shared experiences, both challenging and rewarding, forge a deep camaraderie that transcends words.

This bond strengthens their sense of unity, making them an effective and cohesive group in their mission. They draw inspiration from their shared passion for the catacombs and the knowledge that their work contributes to preserving a priceless piece of Parisian history.

SECRETS OF THE BONE LABYRINTH: THE HAUNTED CATACOMBS OF PARIS

Silent reverence fills the air as the Cataflics carry out their patrols. Within the catacombs, time stands still, and the guardians honor the final resting place of those who have long departed the world above.

In their silent vigil, the Cataflics pay homage to the deceased and the catacombs' historical significance. The solemnity of their presence echoes through the limestone walls, ensuring that the catacombs remain undisturbed by unauthorized visitors.

The Cataflics' legacy lies in the shadows, concealed from the public eye. Yet, their impact on preserving the Catacombs of Paris is immeasurable. Their dedicated efforts, silent vigilance, and unyielding commitment ensure that the haunting secrets and architectural wonders of the Bone Labyrinth endure.

For generations to come, the Cataflics will remain an integral part of the catacombs' lore, a symbol of guardianship and reverence for this underground necropolis. Their presence adds an air of enigma to the catacombs' mystique, perpetuating the Secrets of the Haunted Catacombs of Paris and the guardians who watch over them.

As long as the Catacombs of Paris endure, the Cataflics' eternal watch will continue. Their unyielding dedication to protecting this historical site from trespassers and preserving its sanctity ensures that the haunting secrets of the catacombs remain shrouded in mystery and reverence.

The Cataflics will continue to walk in silence through the subterranean realm, serving as the unseen guardians of the catacombs' history, its past, and its future. They stand as a testament to the enduring devotion to preserving the architectural wonders and haunting allure of the Bone Labyrinth - the Secrets of the Haunted Catacombs of Paris.

SECRETS OF THE BONE LABYRINTH: THE HAUNTED CATACOMBS OF PARIS

Chapter 5: The Ghostly Tales

———

L egend has it that within the depths of the Catacombs of Paris, the skulls of the deceased possess a haunting ability - they whisper to those who dare to listen. Trespassers and urban explorers claim to hear faint whispers echoing through the dark passages, as if the souls of the departed are trying to communicate from beyond the grave.

While skeptics attribute these whispers to the sound of wind or water, the chilling stories of visitors encountering the whispering skulls add to the catacombs' enigma, leaving many wondering if the souls of the deceased still linger within the Bone Labyrinth.

Among the eerie tales that circulate about the Catacombs, one of the most chilling is the legend of the lost wanderers. According to these stories, trespassers who venture into the catacombs without a guide or proper knowledge of the labyrinthine passages become disoriented and lost in the dark expanse.

It is said that these lost souls wander aimlessly through the endless corridors, searching for an escape that never comes. Their desperate footsteps echo through the catacombs, forever trapped in the underground world, a haunting reminder of the perils of unauthorized exploration.

Some who claim to have encountered the Cataflics describe an eerie figure cloaked in darkness, moving silently through the catacombs like a phantom. This legend of the Phantom Guardian adds to the mystique of the guardians, fueling speculation that they possess otherworldly abilities.

Rumors of the Phantom Guardian tell of a spectral figure that appears and disappears without a trace, haunting those who venture into the catacombs illegally. Whether a product of overactive imaginations or an actual guardian shrouded in legend, the Phantom Guardian adds an air of supernatural intrigue to the Catacombs of Paris.

According to some accounts, late at night, the catacombs come alive with a ghostly procession of shadowy figures. Visitors who have explored the catacombs after dark claim to have witnessed spectral forms moving silently through the passageways.

These ghostly figures are said to be the souls of the deceased, reenacting their final journey as they were brought to rest within the Bone Labyrinth. The chilling apparitions add to the catacombs' aura of mystery, leaving many to wonder if the past is still alive within the underground realm.

A legend that has persisted for centuries tells of a curse that befalls those who disrespect the catacombs or disturb the remains of the deceased. According to this chilling tale, trespassers who disregard the sanctity of the catacombs will be cursed, haunted by vengeful spirits and plagued by misfortune.

Some stories speak of those who have allegedly faced calamities after trespassing into the catacombs, attributing their misfortunes to the curse. Whether a warning to deter unauthorized exploration or a cautionary tale of supernatural consequences, the Curse of the Catacombs serves as a chilling reminder of the catacombs' sacred nature.

Within the catacombs, there are rumors of a mysterious enchanted portal hidden among the walls. This portal is said to be a gateway to another world, where time stands still and the living and the dead coexist.

Legends speak of those who have stumbled upon the enchanted portal, only to find themselves transported to an otherworldly realm. Whether these tales are the products of overactive imaginations or genuine encounters with the supernatural, the legend of the Enchanted Portal adds a tantalizing layer of intrigue to the catacombs' haunting allure.

Among the legends that circulate about the Catacombs, there are stories of a phantom cataphile - an elusive figure who navigates the underground passages with uncanny skill and knowledge. It is said that this mysterious individual appears and disappears like a specter, leaving no trace of their presence.

The legend of the Phantom Cataphile fuels rumors that there are those who have mastered the catacombs' labyrinth and roam the underground world undetected. Whether an urban legend or a true enigma, the Phantom Cataphile adds a touch of mystery to the catacombs' ghost stories.

Some accounts tell of a ghostly spectacle that occurs during certain times of the year, when the veil between the living and the dead is said to be at its thinnest. Witnesses claim to have seen apparitions of long-deceased Parisians, dressed in the fashion of their time, wandering through the catacombs in a haunting parade.

This ghostly procession is said to be a transient glimpse into the past, providing those who witness it with an ethereal connection to the history of the catacombs and the city above. Such stories perpetuate the belief that the catacombs hold secrets that transcend time itself.

Collectively, these chilling legends and ghost stories create an aura of mystery and fear that surrounds the Catacombs of Paris. The Bone Labyrinth becomes a place where the living and the dead seem to intertwine, where the past lingers in the shadows, and where the secrets of the catacombs remain locked in the haunting realm of legend.

As visitors explore the catacombs, they cannot help but wonder if the chilling tales are mere figments of imagination or if the ghostly specters still roam the underground world, guarding its secrets and adding to the enigmatic allure of the Haunted Catacombs of Paris.

Explore first-hand accounts of paranormal encounters from visitors and Catacombs explorers.

One of the most enduring ghostly legends surrounding the Catacombs of Paris is that of the Lady in White. According to the tales, the ghost of a young woman in a flowing white dress is said to wander the underground passages, her presence accompanied by an eerie glow.

SECRETS OF THE BONE LABYRINTH: THE HAUNTED CATACOMBS OF PARIS

Witnesses claim to have glimpsed the Lady in White during their expeditions through the catacombs, but when they try to approach her, she vanishes into the darkness. Some believe that she may be the spirit of a lost soul or a tragic figure from Parisian history, forever seeking solace in the depths of the Bone Labyrinth.

In the darkest recesses of the catacombs, there are chilling accounts of disembodied cries and mournful wails that echo through the air. Visitors have reported feeling an overwhelming sense of sorrow and despair, as if the very walls are imbued with the anguish of the deceased.

Some speculate that these haunting cries are the echoes of long-forgotten souls, trapped in a perpetual state of torment. The eerie chorus of the cries of the damned adds to the catacombs' reputation as a place of sorrow and the unknown.

Among the ghostly legends, one of the most unsettling is that of the shadow figures that dart through the catacombs' darkness. Witnesses have reported seeing fleeting glimpses of shadowy apparitions moving along the walls or lurking in the corners of their vision.

These enigmatic figures are said to be the souls of the deceased, lingering in the catacombs and observing those who intrude upon their resting place. The shadow figures, shrouded in mystery, leave many visitors with an unsettling feeling of being watched, even in the deepest reaches of the Bone Labyrinth.

Some who have ventured into the catacombs claim to have experienced inexplicable occurrences - objects moving on their own, sudden gusts of wind, or strange noises that seem to defy explanation. These incidents have led to stories of mischievous poltergeists haunting the underground world.

According to these legends, the poltergeists are playful spirits, pulling pranks on unsuspecting visitors. While skeptics may attribute these occurrences to natural phenomena or tricks of the mind, the tales of poltergeist pranks add a touch of supernatural intrigue to the catacombs' mysteries.

Amidst the haunting legends, some tales speak of benevolent guardian spirits watching over the catacombs. These spirits are said to be the protectors of the Bone Labyrinth, guiding lost wanderers to safety and shielding visitors from harm.

According to these stories, those who show respect for the catacombs and its history may receive the blessings of the guardian spirits, offering protection and good fortune. The concept of benevolent entities adds a glimmer of hope and positivity to the otherwise eerie atmosphere of the catacombs.

The Catacombs of Paris have long been associated with spiritual and supernatural phenomena, leading some to believe that the underground realm serves as a portal to the beyond. According to these legends, the catacombs act as a conduit between the world of the living and the realm of the dead.

As visitors explore the catacombs, they may unknowingly cross the threshold between the physical and the spiritual, inviting encounters with the unknown. The concept of the catacombs as a portal to the beyond infuses the Bone Labyrinth with an element of mysticism and serves as a reminder of the delicate balance between life and death.

The chilling legends and ghost stories that shroud the Catacombs of Paris contribute to the enduring sense of restlessness that pervades the underground realm. The catacombs, with their haunting allure and enigmatic secrets, leave visitors and guardians alike contemplating the mysteries that lie within the darkened passages.

Whether these legends are the product of centuries of imagination or hints of the supernatural, they continue to weave an enthralling tapestry of mystery and intrigue around the catacombs. The Bone Labyrinth remains an eternal enigma, inviting visitors to explore its haunted depths and uncover the Secrets of the Haunted Catacombs of Paris.

EDWARD TURNER

Chapter 6: The Lost Souls

The origins of the Catacombs of Paris can be traced back to ancient times when the area now known as Paris was known as Lutetia, a Roman settlement. The region was abundant in limestone, and the Romans excavated vast quarries beneath the city to extract this valuable building material.

Over the centuries, the limestone was used in the construction of various iconic structures in Paris, including the Notre-Dame Cathedral and the Louvre Palace. As the quarries were dug deeper and expanded, they formed an intricate network of underground tunnels and galleries.

During the medieval period, Paris faced an escalating problem with overcrowded cemeteries within the city walls. The churchyards, such as the Cemetery of the Innocents, had become saturated with graves, leading to unsanitary conditions and the spread of diseases.

In 1780, a series of unfortunate incidents highlighted the urgency of the situation. The collapse of a wall in the Cemetery of the Innocents exposed a mass of decomposing corpses, creating a public health crisis. The authorities were forced to take action to address the pressing issue of overburdened cemeteries.

In response to the crisis, it was decided to relocate the remains from the overcrowded cemeteries to the abandoned quarries beneath the city. Between 1786 and 1788, a systematic transfer of bones took place, and the remains of approximately six million people were carefully and respectfully transported to the Catacombs.

The task of relocating the bones was carried out with great care and reverence. The remains were arranged in a macabre yet artful manner, creating the haunting ossuary that visitors encounter today.

The relocation of the bones not only solved the problem of overcrowded cemeteries but also served to create an ossuary that would become an enduring symbol of Parisian history. The Catacombs were not initially intended as a place for public visitation, but their unique nature and historical significance eventually drew the curiosity of Parisians and visitors alike.

In 1809, the Catacombs were officially opened to the public, marking the beginning of their transformation from a mere storage place for bones to a site of curiosity and fascination. Over the years, the Catacombs evolved into a haunting attraction, attracting curious explorers, writers, and artists seeking inspiration from their eerie beauty.

The Catacombs of Paris became a place of remembrance and veneration for the deceased, offering a unique space where the living could connect with the past. As visitors descended into the depths of the Bone Labyrinth, they were confronted with the vastness of human mortality and the transient nature of life.

SECRETS OF THE BONE LABYRINTH: THE HAUNTED CATACOMBS OF PARIS

The catacombs served as a poignant reminder of the shared human experience, transcending social and cultural boundaries. The bones of people from all walks of life were interred side by side, creating a sense of unity and shared destiny in death.

The Catacombs of Paris stand as a solemn testament to the historical tragedies and challenges faced by the city. The relocation of the bones was a response to the perils of epidemic diseases and unsanitary conditions in medieval Paris.

Additionally, the Catacombs also bear witness to the cataclysmic events of the French Revolution. During this tumultuous period, the catacombs served as a refuge and hiding place for revolutionaries, contributing to their rich historical tapestry.

Throughout the centuries, the Catacombs of Paris have evolved to become more than a mere ossuary. They are now a cultural and historical symbol, representing the resilience of the city and its people in the face of adversity.

The Catacombs are a place where the past and present intertwine, where the echoes of history resonate through the limestone walls. They continue to capture the imagination of people from all over the world, drawing them into the haunting secrets of the Bone Labyrinth and the captivating stories that lie within.

Today, the Catacombs of Paris remain a protected historical site, carefully preserved to retain their cultural and architectural significance. The Cataflics, as the guardians of this subterranean realm, play a crucial role in ensuring that the catacombs remain a place of respect, reverence, and historical preservation.

As visitors descend into the haunting depths of the Catacombs, they step into a living museum that chronicles the history of Paris and the triumphs and tragedies of its past. The Catacombs of Paris stand as a poignant reminder of the impermanence of life and the enduring importance of preserving the stories of those who came before us.

Over the years, the Catacombs of Paris have captured the imaginations of writers, artists, and filmmakers, who have drawn inspiration from its eerie beauty and haunting history. The catacombs have been featured in various literary works, paintings, and movies, further solidifying their place in popular culture.

From the haunting tales of Edgar Allan Poe to the evocative paintings of Édouard Manet, the Catacombs have left an indelible mark on the artistic landscape. Their dark allure and mysterious ambiance have become a symbol of the macabre, providing artists with a unique canvas to explore themes of mortality and the human condition.

During World War II, the Catacombs of Paris served as a refuge for both civilians and members of the French Resistance. The underground tunnels offered a place of shelter and safety during the German occupation of Paris, allowing people to escape the dangers of the surface.

SECRETS OF THE BONE LABYRINTH: THE HAUNTED CATACOMBS OF PARIS

The catacombs became a network of resistance hideouts, providing secret meeting places and storage for weapons and supplies. The courage and resourcefulness of those who sought refuge in the Catacombs during these tumultuous times added another layer of historical significance to the Bone Labyrinth.

Today, the Catacombs of Paris remain open to the public, attracting tourists and history enthusiasts from around the world. The Cataflics continue their sacred duty of guarding the underground realm, preserving its sanctity and protecting it from unauthorized exploration.

Visitors to the Catacombs have the opportunity to delve into the enigmatic history of Paris, connecting with the past through the bones of those who rest within the underground ossuary. The catacombs offer a somber and reflective experience, inviting contemplation on the impermanence of life and the importance of cherishing our shared human heritage.

The Catacombs of Paris have withstood the test of time, surviving wars, revolutions, and the passing of centuries. As a symbol of resilience, the catacombs stand as a reminder of the enduring spirit of Paris and its people.

They are a testament to the city's ability to adapt and transform, from ancient quarries to a resting place for millions of bones, and eventually becoming a haunting historical site of fascination and wonder. The Catacombs represent the city's capacity to face challenges and transform them into opportunities for preservation and commemoration.

Beyond their chilling legends and ghost stories, the Catacombs of Paris offer valuable lessons to the modern world. They remind us of the importance of preserving historical sites and cultural heritage for future generations.

The Catacombs serve as a poignant reminder of the impact of epidemic diseases and the importance of public health measures. They prompt us to reflect on our own mortality and the fleeting nature of life, encouraging us to live with purpose and appreciation.

As visitors explore the Catacombs of Paris, they are called to approach with reverence and respect for the souls that rest within. The catacombs are not merely a tourist attraction; they are a sacred space that houses the memories of millions.

In a world often preoccupied with the rush of modern life, the Catacombs offer a solemn sanctuary for introspection and remembrance. They are a place to pay homage to the past, to the lives lived, and to honor the legacies that continue to shape the world today.

The haunting allure of the Catacombs of Paris endures, drawing visitors into its depths with a blend of curiosity and trepidation. The chilling legends, historical events, and tragic tales that have shaped the Bone Labyrinth continue to captivate the imagination and weave a rich tapestry of human history.

As the Cataflics continue their silent vigil in the underground realm, the secrets of the Catacombs remain guarded and shrouded in mystery. The Bone Labyrinth stands as a timeless

SECRETS OF THE BONE LABYRINTH: THE HAUNTED CATACOMBS OF PARIS

monument to the past, a place where the veil between the living and the dead seems to blur, and where the echoes of history resonate in the darkness. The Catacombs of Paris, with their secrets of the past, are an enduring reminder of the enigmatic nature of the human experience and the enduring allure of the unknown.

The ossuary within the Catacombs of Paris holds immense significance as a place of commemoration and remembrance. It serves as the final resting place for the remains of millions of Parisians, carefully arranged and preserved to honor their memory.

As visitors descend into the Bone Labyrinth, they are confronted with the bones of the deceased, creating a somber and reflective atmosphere. The ossuary stands as a poignant reminder of the impermanence of life and the universal nature of mortality, inviting contemplation on the transience of human existence.

The macabre symbolism of the ossuary lies in its visual representation of death. The carefully stacked bones, arranged in decorative patterns, create a striking and haunting tableau. Skulls, femurs, and other skeletal remains form walls that stretch into darkness, evoking a sense of mortality that transcends time and space.

The ossuary's macabre symbolism challenges visitors to confront the inevitability of death and serves as a memento mori - a reminder of their own mortality and the fleeting nature of life.

Beyond its historical significance, the ossuary of the Catacombs prompts visitors to reflect on the human condition. The remains of those interred within the Bone Labyrinth represent a diverse cross-section of society - men, women, children, rich, poor, nobility, and commoners.

In this shared resting place, social distinctions are erased, emphasizing the commonality of human experience. The ossuary serves as a powerful reminder of the shared fate that unites all people, regardless of their backgrounds or circumstances.

The ossuary's macabre symbolism also serves as a symbol of unity. Within its walls, the bones of millions are intermingled, side by side, without regard to status or wealth. In death, all are equal, and the ossuary stands as a testament to the unifying force of mortality.

This symbolic unity challenges visitors to contemplate the connections that bind humanity together, transcending individual differences and emphasizing the shared journey of life and death.

The macabre symbolism of the ossuary carries with it a profound lesson in transience. The human remains within the Catacombs remind visitors of the impermanence of life and the fleeting nature of human existence.

The bones of those who once walked the streets of Paris now rest in eternal silence within the ossuary. This lesson in transience urges visitors to cherish the moments of life, embrace the present, and acknowledge the inevitable passage of time.

The ossuary's macabre symbolism provides an opportunity for visitors to confront their own mortality. As they walk through the Catacombs, they come face to face with the bones of those who came before them, forcing them to acknowledge the reality of death and their own place within the continuum of time.

Confronting mortality in this way can be a deeply transformative and introspective experience, prompting visitors to reevaluate their priorities and find meaning in the fleeting moments of life.

The macabre symbolism of the ossuary within the Catacombs has inspired countless artists and writers throughout history. From painters to poets, the haunting allure of the Bone Labyrinth has served as a muse for creative expression.

Artists have captured the eerie beauty of the ossuary in their paintings and sculptures, while writers have woven chilling tales and introspective narratives centered around the Catacombs. The macabre symbolism of the ossuary has become a recurring motif in art and literature, evoking themes of mortality, human frailty, and the enigmatic nature of existence.

The ossuary invites visitors to step into a realm of contemplation and introspection. The macabre symbolism and somber atmosphere encourage moments of silence and reflection, where visitors can ponder the mysteries of life and death, the passage of time, and the significance of their own journey.

In this meditative space, the ossuary becomes more than just a collection of bones; it transforms into a sacred and meaningful site for personal introspection and philosophical exploration.

The ossuary's macabre symbolism also encapsulates the paradoxical relationship between beauty and death. Despite the chilling nature of the Catacombs, visitors often find themselves captivated by the haunting beauty of the carefully arranged bones and the intricate patterns they form.

The ossuary challenges conventional notions of beauty, demonstrating that even in the presence of death and decay, there can be a haunting allure that transcends the macabre.

Ultimately, the significance of the ossuary lies in its ability to preserve and commemorate the history of Paris and its people. The bones within the Catacombs serve as tangible relics of the past, offering a living connection to the stories and memories of those who lived and died in the city centuries ago.

Through its macabre symbolism, the ossuary becomes a powerful testament to the enduring nature of human memory and the indelible impact that people leave on the world even after they have passed away.

As visitors traverse the Catacombs of Paris and behold the ossuary's macabre symbolism, they are reminded of the cyclical nature of life and death, the impermanence of human existence, and the enduring power of memory. The haunting allure of the Catacombs continues to captivate the imagination and evoke a deep sense of reflection, ensuring that the macabre symbolism of the ossuary remains etched in the hearts and minds of all who venture into the depths of the Bone Labyrinth.

The macabre symbolism of the ossuary within the Catacombs has the remarkable ability to transform fear into fascination. While the initial descent into the underground realm may evoke feelings of trepidation, visitors often find themselves drawn deeper into the Bone Labyrinth, captivated by its eerie beauty and historical significance.

As they wander amidst the carefully stacked bones, fear gives way to a profound sense of awe and wonder. The macabre symbolism becomes a gateway to contemplation, encouraging visitors to embrace the mysteries of life and death with curiosity and respect.

Confronted with the macabre symbolism of the ossuary, visitors are compelled to confront their own mortality. This confrontation can be both sobering and liberating, encouraging individuals to embrace life more fully and to appreciate the preciousness of every moment.

The Catacombs offer a unique opportunity for existential introspection, as the bones of those who came before serve as silent reminders of the transitory nature of human existence. Through this confrontation, visitors may find solace in accepting the inevitability of death as an integral part of the human experience.

The ossuary's macabre symbolism harkens back to ancient traditions of memento mori and vanitas, themes prevalent in art and philosophy throughout history. The Catacombs of Paris, with its solemn display of bones, embody the timeless wisdom of these traditions.

In an era where modern society often seeks to avoid discussions of death and mortality, the macabre symbolism of the ossuary offers a valuable reminder of the wisdom of the ancients. It encourages individuals to confront their mortality, embrace the impermanence of life, and find meaning in the transient nature of human existence.

The ossuary's macabre symbolism instills a sense of humility and reverence in those who venture into the Catacombs. As visitors stand amidst the bones of millions, they are humbled by the magnitude of human history and the collective journey of those who came before.

The Catacombs offer a sanctuary for reflection and meditation, inspiring individuals to approach the mysteries of life and death with a sense of awe and respect. In this subterranean realm, the macabre symbolism serves as a guide to contemplation, urging visitors to embrace the solemnity of the ossuary and the profound truths it represents.

Beyond its historical significance, the macabre symbolism of the ossuary carries an enduring legacy of the unknown. Despite the meticulous efforts to identify and transfer the remains, many of the bones within the Catacombs remain unattributed to specific individuals.

SECRETS OF THE BONE LABYRINTH: THE HAUNTED CATACOMBS OF PARIS

This legacy of the unknown adds a layer of mystery to the ossuary, reminding visitors of the countless stories and experiences that lie obscured in the depths of the Bone Labyrinth. The macabre symbolism becomes a poignant reminder of the vastness of human history and the inexhaustible stories of those who remain anonymous but not forgotten.

Ultimately, the macabre symbolism of the ossuary serves as a profound teacher for the living. It beckons visitors to embrace the present and to recognize the significance of life in the face of death.

Through its haunting beauty and historical resonance, the ossuary inspires individuals to live with purpose and meaning, to cherish the relationships that enrich their lives, and to contribute to a legacy that will endure beyond their mortal existence.

The macabre symbolism of the ossuary within the Catacombs of Paris remains a source of enduring fascination and intrigue. Its chilling allure challenges visitors to confront their own mortality, find solace in the impermanence of life, and embrace the profound interconnectedness of humanity.

Through the macabre symbolism of the ossuary, the Catacombs continue to hold a mirror to the human condition, reflecting the essence of existence itself. The Bone Labyrinth stands as a testament to the eternal dance between life and death, inviting visitors to explore the haunting beauty and enigmatic symbolism that lies within the depths of the Catacombs of Paris.

SECRETS OF THE BONE LABYRINTH: THE HAUNTED CATACOMBS OF PARIS

Chapter 7: The Curse of the Catacombs

The alleged curse associated with disturbing the bones and relics of the Catacombs of Paris has its roots in both historical events and superstitions. When the catacombs were first transformed into an ossuary, it was intended as a solution to the overcrowding of cemeteries and to honor the deceased. However, the process of moving millions of bones and remains also involved disturbing the resting places of countless individuals.

Some believe that the disturbed spirits of those whose remains were relocated could not find peace and rest, leading to the creation of the curse. Additionally, the catacombs' eerie atmosphere and haunting legends contributed to the perception of the catacombs as a place of dark energy and spiritual unrest.

One aspect of the alleged curse revolves around the belief in guardian spirits protecting the Catacombs of Paris. According to this legend, ancient spirits dwell within the depths of the ossuary, guarding its sanctity and ensuring that those who disturb the bones face consequences for their actions.

These guardian spirits are said to be vengeful and protective of the catacombs, seeking retribution against those who desecrate their resting place. This belief has acted as a deterrent, discouraging some from attempting to explore or tamper with the catacombs without proper authorization.

Throughout history, there have been tales of misfortune befalling those who have dared to disturb the bones and relics of the Catacombs. Stories of accidents, injuries, and unexplained occurrences have circulated, adding to the belief in the curse.

These tales often involve individuals experiencing bad luck, accidents, or encountering supernatural occurrences shortly after visiting or disturbing the catacombs. While skeptics attribute these incidents to coincidence or suggest a psychological effect, the belief in the curse persists, influencing the perception of the catacombs as a place of mystery and danger.

The alleged curse associated with the Catacombs of Paris has become a popular theme in literature, films, and urban legends. Writers and filmmakers have drawn on the haunting allure of the catacombs and the belief in the curse to create captivating narratives filled with supernatural elements and eerie twists.

Urban legends abound with stories of adventurers and explorers who ventured into the catacombs against warnings, only to face dire consequences as a result of disturbing the bones. These tales, whether based on real incidents or pure fiction, contribute to the enduring mystique of the Catacombs and the notion of an ancient curse guarding its secrets.

The belief in curses and superstitions is often fueled by the power of suggestion. The macabre symbolism and haunting atmosphere of the Catacombs of Paris can evoke a sense of dread and unease in some visitors. When combined with stories of the alleged curse, the power of suggestion can further reinforce the perception that the catacombs are a place to be approached with caution and respect.

In some cases, the belief in the curse can influence behavior, dissuading individuals from engaging in disrespectful or unauthorized activities within the catacombs out of fear of potential consequences.

While the belief in the curse of the Catacombs of Paris is widely held, rational explanations for the alleged misfortunes and accidents can be attributed to natural factors. The catacombs, as an underground labyrinth with low lighting and uneven terrain, pose inherent risks to explorers and visitors.

Accidents or injuries may occur due to tripping or falling on the uneven ground, and the dim lighting can lead to disorientation and potential hazards. Additionally, the catacombs' popularity as a tourist attraction increases the likelihood of accidents due to overcrowding and the potential for tourists not following safety guidelines.

Regardless of the belief in the curse, the legend surrounding the Catacombs of Paris serves as a powerful reminder of the importance of respecting historical and sacred sites. As a resting place for millions of souls, the catacombs hold deep significance and historical value.

Visitors are encouraged to approach the catacombs with reverence and respect, recognizing the sanctity of the space and the memory of those who rest within. By honoring the past and treating the catacombs with care, visitors can participate in preserving its historical and cultural significance for future generations.

The alleged curse associated with disturbing the bones and relics of the Catacombs of Paris has become a part of the storied history of this underground realm. Whether rooted in historical events, spiritual beliefs, or popular imagination, the belief in the curse adds to the haunting allure and enigmatic reputation of the catacombs.

As visitors explore the Bone Labyrinth, the legends and superstitions surrounding the catacombs continue to captivate the imagination, drawing them into a realm of mystery and fascination. The alleged curse becomes a symbolic reminder of the profound connection between the living and the deceased, and a testament to the enduring power of the human psyche to find meaning and wonder in the unknown.

The alleged curse surrounding the Catacombs of Paris also highlights the importance of cultural preservation and respect for historical sites. The ossuary holds immense historical and cultural significance, serving as a tangible link to Paris's past and the lives of countless individuals who once walked its streets.

The belief in the curse acts as a cautionary tale, reminding visitors and explorers that these are not just dark and mysterious tunnels, but a place of profound human history and collective memory. Respecting the sanctity of the catacombs ensures that its cultural value and the stories of those interred within are preserved for future generations.

———————

AS WITH MANY LEGENDS and curses, the alleged curse of the Catacombs of Paris blurs the line between myth and reality. While some may dismiss it as mere superstition, others find intrigue and fascination in the possibility of supernatural forces at play.

The tale of the curse persists in part due to the catacombs' reputation as a place of mystery and the unknown. It reflects humanity's enduring fascination with the afterlife and the mysteries that lie beyond the realm of the living.

The alleged curse surrounding the Catacombs also showcases the power of the human imagination to create and perpetuate stories. Over time, the catacombs have become enshrouded in a tapestry of legends, each adding to the aura of mystery that surrounds the Bone Labyrinth.

These tales of curses and guardian spirits offer a glimpse into the human psyche, where fear, fascination, and curiosity intertwine to create a captivating narrative. The power of storytelling, passed down through generations, ensures that the legend of the curse endures, adding to the catacombs' allure.

While some may dismiss the alleged curse as mere folklore, it serves as a reminder of the importance of responsible exploration and tourism. The catacombs' popularity as a tourist attraction can lead to overcrowding and potential harm to the site if visitors do not follow guidelines or exhibit respect for the space.

The legend of the curse encourages visitors to approach the catacombs with a sense of mindfulness and responsibility. By adhering to safety protocols and respecting the sanctity of the site, visitors can ensure the preservation of the catacombs for future generations to explore and appreciate.

Ultimately, the alleged curse adds to the enigmatic allure of the Catacombs of Paris. The Bone Labyrinth stands as a testament to the mysteries of history and the enduring fascination with death and the afterlife.

As visitors descend into the dark passages, the legend of the curse lingers in the back of their minds, heightening their sense of adventure and trepidation. The catacombs become a place of exploration, reflection, and contemplation, inviting visitors to embrace the haunting beauty and historical significance that lies within.

Despite the alleged curse and the chilling legends that surround the catacombs, it has endured as a symbol of resilience and continuity. Over the centuries, the Bone Labyrinth has witnessed wars, revolutions, and the passage of time, yet it remains an integral part of Parisian history and culture.

The catacombs' enduring allure, coupled with the belief in the curse, has ensured that its story continues to be passed down through generations. This resilience is a testament to the power of human storytelling and the enduring fascination with the mysteries of the past.

In the end, the alleged curse of the Catacombs of Paris serves as an invitation to wonder and contemplation. As visitors walk among the bones of the departed, they are encouraged to consider the interconnectedness of humanity and the impermanence of life.

The Bone Labyrinth invites individuals to explore the depths of history and embrace the unknown, reminding us that there is still much to be discovered and appreciated in the world around us. The legend of the curse is just one facet of the catacombs' multifaceted allure, drawing visitors into a realm of fascination and mystery.

The alleged curse associated with disturbing the bones and relics of the Catacombs of Paris weaves a tapestry of myths and reality. Rooted in historical events and the human imagination, the belief in the curse adds to the haunting allure and enigmatic reputation of the Bone Labyrinth.

Whether perceived as folklore or a cautionary tale, the legend of the curse serves as a reminder of the importance of cultural preservation, respect for historical sites, and responsible exploration. It invites visitors to delve into the depths of the Catacombs with curiosity, respect, and a willingness to embrace the mysteries of history and the human experience. In the end, the Catacombs of Paris remain a timeless monument to the past, where the whispers of the departed continue to echo through the corridors of time.

The stories of misfortune and tragedy experienced by those who have defied the warnings and ventured into the Catacombs of Paris without proper authorization or respect for the space serve as cautionary tales, reinforcing the belief in the alleged curse and the need for responsible exploration.

1. Accidents and Injuries: Many of the stories involve accidents and injuries befalling those who have disregarded safety guidelines or ventured into restricted areas. The Catacombs are an underground labyrinth with uneven terrain, low lighting, and hidden hazards, making them inherently dangerous for unauthorized exploration. Tales of individuals tripping, falling, or getting lost in the dark passages emphasize the importance of caution and preparedness.

2. Getting Lost: The Catacombs of Paris form an intricate network of tunnels spanning several kilometers. For those who venture off designated paths or enter without a guide, it is easy to become disoriented and lost in the labyrinthine passages. Getting lost in the dark and claustrophobic catacombs can be a terrifying experience, and some stories recount individuals spending hours trying to find their way back to the exit.

3. Paranormal Experiences: The eerie atmosphere of the Catacombs has led some to believe they have had paranormal experiences during their unauthorized explorations. Tales of hearing disembodied voices, seeing apparitions, or feeling an inexplicable sense of dread add to the belief that the catacombs are haunted and guarded by unseen forces.

SECRETS OF THE BONE LABYRINTH: THE HAUNTED CATACOMBS OF PARIS

4. Arrests and Legal Consequences: The Catacombs of Paris are protected by strict laws and regulations, and entering without authorization can result in legal consequences. Some stories involve individuals being caught by the Cataflics or the police while attempting to explore the catacombs illegally. Trespassers have faced fines, legal proceedings, and even deportation, emphasizing the importance of respecting the rules and guidelines in place.

5. Psychological Effects: The darkness, silence, and oppressive atmosphere of the catacombs can have psychological effects on some individuals. Being surrounded by millions of bones and contemplating mortality can evoke feelings of anxiety, fear, and unease. For those who are unprepared for the experience, it can be overwhelming and emotionally distressing.

6. Vandalism and Disrespect: Unfortunately, some stories involve individuals who have ventured into the catacombs with a lack of respect for the sanctity of the space. Instances of vandalism, graffiti, and the desecration of bones have been reported, causing outrage among those who value the historical and cultural significance of the Catacombs.

7. Safety Rescues: Occasionally, authorities are called to conduct safety rescues for individuals who become lost or injured while exploring the catacombs. These operations can be challenging and risky, as the underground tunnels are narrow and treacherous, making it difficult to reach those in need of assistance.

8. Lost and Never Found: Some of the most tragic stories involve individuals who have ventured into the Catacombs and never returned. Despite extensive search and rescue efforts, these explorers have seemingly disappeared without a trace, adding an air of mystery and tragedy to their fate. The vastness of the Catacombs and the complexity of its passages make it challenging to locate missing individuals, leaving families and friends with unanswered questions and unresolved grief.

9. Health Hazards: The underground environment of the Catacombs presents health hazards that can lead to serious consequences for trespassers. The lack of proper ventilation can lead to a buildup of toxic gases, putting explorers at risk of suffocation or poisoning. The damp and humid conditions can also promote the growth of mold and fungi, which can cause respiratory issues and other health problems.

10. Collapses and Structural Instability: The Catacombs of Paris are located beneath the city, and their structures are subject to the pressures of the surrounding urban environment. Stories of sections of the catacombs collapsing or becoming structurally unstable serve as a stark reminder of the dangers of entering these underground tunnels without proper authorization or expertise.

11. Encounters with Authorities: The Catacombs are closely monitored by authorities, and those caught trespassing can face serious consequences. While some may attempt to evade the Cataflics or police, stories of individuals being confronted by these guardians of the catacombs highlight the seriousness of unauthorized exploration. Encounters with the authorities can

lead to legal consequences and tarnish the experience of those who sought to explore the catacombs illicitly.

12. Regret and Emotional Impact: Beyond the physical dangers and legal ramifications, many stories recount the emotional impact and regret experienced by those who have defied the warnings and explored the Catacombs without authorization. Some trespassers have expressed remorse for their actions, realizing the disrespect they showed to the resting place of the deceased and the potential harm they caused to themselves and others.

13. Cultural Disrespect and Preservation Concerns: The Catacombs of Paris are not only a historical site but also a place of cultural significance and remembrance. Stories of vandalism and disrespect toward the bones and relics underscore the need for cultural preservation and respect for heritage sites. Such actions not only defile the sanctity of the catacombs but also threaten the preservation of this historical and cultural treasure for future generations.

14. Impact on Local Community: The unauthorized exploration of the catacombs can have an impact on the local community and those living near the entrances. Noise, littering, and other disruptive behaviors by trespassers can lead to tensions and grievances among residents who value the tranquility and cultural significance of the Catacombs.

The stories of misfortune and tragedy experienced by those who have defied the warnings and explored the Catacombs of Paris without proper authorization paint a sobering picture of the potential risks and consequences of such actions. From physical dangers to legal repercussions and emotional impacts, these cautionary tales serve as reminders of the importance of respecting historical sites, following safety guidelines, and preserving cultural heritage. The alleged curse surrounding the catacombs further reinforces the aura of mystery and respect surrounding this underground realm, discouraging some from engaging in unauthorized exploration and adding to the enduring fascination and enigmatic allure of the Bone Labyrinth.

SECRETS OF THE BONE LABYRINTH: THE HAUNTED CATACOMBS OF PARIS

Chapter 8: Paranormal Investigations

―――

Scientific Investigations:

1. Archaeological Studies: Archaeologists have conducted extensive studies within the Catacombs of Paris to gain insights into the historical and cultural aspects of the site. Excavations have revealed valuable information about burial practices, the demographics of the people interred, and the social and economic conditions of Paris during different periods.

2. Anthropological Research: Anthropologists have studied the human remains found within the catacombs to better understand the health, diet, and living conditions of past populations. Through the analysis of skeletal remains, they have uncovered valuable data on disease prevalence, life expectancy, and the impact of urbanization on human health.

3. Geological Surveys: Geologists have explored the catacombs to study the geological composition of the limestone tunnels and to assess the structural stability of the underground network. Their findings contribute to the preservation and maintenance of this historical site and help identify potential risks such as collapses or subsidence.

4. Environmental Studies: Environmental scientists have monitored the underground microclimate of the catacombs to study the effects of humidity, temperature, and air quality on

the preservation of the bones and relics. Understanding the environmental factors that impact the catacombs is crucial for their long-term conservation.

5. Biodiversity Studies: The Catacombs of Paris host unique subterranean ecosystems, including certain species of fungi and other microorganisms. Scientists have conducted biodiversity studies to explore the life forms that thrive in the dark and nutrient-rich environment of the catacombs, shedding light on the potential ecological implications of underground urban spaces.

Supernatural Investigations:

1. Paranormal Studies: Due to the catacombs' eerie reputation and ghostly legends, paranormal investigators have explored the site in search of supernatural phenomena. These investigations involve using specialized equipment such as EVP (Electronic Voice Phenomena) recorders and infrared cameras to capture potential paranormal activity.

2. Psychic and Medium Sessions: Some individuals claim to have psychic or mediumistic abilities that enable them to communicate with spirits or detect energy anomalies. Psychic and medium sessions have been conducted within the catacombs to establish contact with the departed souls and to seek answers to lingering mysteries.

3. Séances and Rituals: Occultists and practitioners of various spiritual traditions have conducted séances and rituals within the catacombs, believing that the underground space enhances their connection to the spiritual realm. These activities often

aim to appease or communicate with the spirits believed to dwell within the catacombs.

4. Ghost Tours and Haunted Experiences: For tourists seeking an adrenaline rush and a glimpse into the supernatural, ghost tours and haunted experiences are offered within the catacombs. These tours combine historical facts with chilling ghost stories to create an atmosphere of mystery and intrigue.

5. Ouija Board Sessions: Ouija boards, also known as spirit boards, have been used by some visitors to attempt communication with spirits within the catacombs. These sessions involve participants placing their hands on a planchette, which then moves to spell out messages believed to come from the spirit world.

The Catacombs of Paris have been subject to both scientific investigations and supernatural explorations. Archaeologists, anthropologists, geologists, and environmental scientists have contributed to the understanding and preservation of this historical site. At the same time, paranormal enthusiasts, psychics, and seekers of the supernatural have engaged in various activities in search of mysteries and connections to the spirit world. These diverse investigations have contributed to the aura of mystery and fascination that continues to surround the Catacombs, making it a place where science and the supernatural coexist in an intricate dance of exploration and wonder.

The line between scientific and supernatural investigations within the Catacombs of Paris can sometimes become blurred, as both realms seek answers to mysteries that lie hidden in the depths of the underground realm. Some scientific researchers may explore the catacombs with an open mind, acknowledging the importance of cultural beliefs and legends in shaping human history.

Similarly, supernatural investigators might draw upon historical and archaeological information to support their claims of paranormal activity, creating a synthesis of knowledge that blurs the boundaries between fact and folklore.

The fame of the Catacombs of Paris as a haunted and mysterious location has fueled a thriving industry of haunted tours and cultural tourism. Tour guides regale visitors with chilling tales of ghostly encounters and supernatural occurrences, weaving historical facts with legends to create an immersive and captivating experience.

While these tours cater to the curiosity and thrill-seeking nature of tourists, they also play a role in preserving the cultural and historical significance of the Catacombs by drawing attention to its past and the stories of those laid to rest within.

The Catacombs' eerie ambiance, dark passageways, and haunting legends can have a profound psychological impact on visitors. The combination of the catacombs' historical significance, supernatural associations, and underground environment can trigger feelings of fear, unease, and wonder.

For some, the experience can be empowering, as they confront their fears and contemplate mortality. Others may find it emotionally distressing, leading to psychological effects that linger long after leaving the Bone Labyrinth.

The belief in the supernatural and the allure of the unknown drive individuals and investigators to seek unexplained phenomena within the catacombs. Whether through psychic communication, séances, or other spiritual practices, some are drawn to the catacombs with the hope of encountering something beyond the realm of scientific explanation.

While skeptics may dismiss such efforts as mere wishful thinking or the power of suggestion, for those who have had unusual experiences or encountered phenomena they cannot explain, the Catacombs of Paris become a place of wonder and mystery that defies rational understanding.

Ultimately, the Catacombs of Paris hold an irresistible allure that blends history and mystery, science and superstition. As visitors and investigators tread upon the bones of the departed, they are surrounded by centuries of human history and the enigmatic stories of those who have come before.

Whether driven by scientific curiosity, a fascination with the supernatural, or a desire to delve into the depths of human existence, the Catacombs continue to beckon people from around the world to explore the ancient and haunting realm hidden beneath the bustling streets of Paris.

The Catacombs of Paris stand as a tapestry of exploration, where scientific investigations and supernatural inquiries interweave to create a complex and captivating narrative. From archaeological studies to ghost tours, each thread contributes to the mystique and allure that surrounds this underground realm.

While some may seek concrete answers through scientific methods, others embrace the enigmatic and embrace the mysteries that the catacombs hold. In this way, the Catacombs of Paris continue to fascinate and captivate, leaving visitors and investigators alike with a profound sense of wonder and a connection to the timeless echoes of the past.

The evidence and theories put forth by researchers and paranormal experts regarding the Catacombs of Paris are diverse and often controversial. While scientific investigations tend to rely on empirical evidence and objective analysis, paranormal experts draw upon personal experiences, eyewitness accounts, and subjective interpretations of phenomena. It is essential to approach these claims with a critical mind, considering the following aspects:

1. Scientific Investigations:

- Archaeological Evidence: Archaeological studies have unearthed valuable information about burial practices, historical context, and the demography of the interred individuals. These findings provide tangible evidence of the catacombs' historical significance and their role as a resting place for millions of Parisians.

- Anthropological Research: Anthropological analysis of the human remains sheds light on the health, lifestyles, and challenges faced by past populations. These studies offer valuable insights into the living conditions and social aspects of the people buried in the catacombs.

- Geological Studies: Geologists' assessments of the catacombs' structure and stability contribute to the preservation and safety of the site. Their findings ensure that potential risks are identified and addressed, helping to maintain the catacombs for future generations.

- Environmental Studies: Environmental scientists monitor the underground microclimate to understand its impact on the preservation of bones and relics. Such studies are crucial for safeguarding the catacombs from environmental degradation.

2. Paranormal Claims:

- Personal Experiences: Paranormal experts and enthusiasts often cite their personal experiences as evidence of supernatural activity within the catacombs. These experiences may include hearing unexplained sounds, witnessing apparitions, or sensing a presence.

- EVP Recordings: Electronic Voice Phenomena (EVP) recordings are often used to capture alleged communication from spirits. These recordings are believed by some to provide auditory evidence of ghostly encounters.

- Psychic and Mediumistic Sessions: Psychics and mediums claim to communicate with spirits residing within the catacombs. Their subjective interpretations and interactions with the spiritual realm form the basis of their paranormal theories.

- Haunting Legends and Ghost Stories: The catacombs' reputation as a haunted site is further fueled by chilling legends and ghost stories. While such tales are not direct evidence of paranormal activity, they contribute to the perception of the catacombs as a place with supernatural significance.

3. Skepticism and Critical Analysis:

Skeptics often question the validity of paranormal claims and emphasize the need for critical analysis. They argue that personal experiences may be influenced by psychological factors such as suggestion or expectation.

Furthermore, they challenge the credibility of EVP recordings, asserting that they can be influenced by background noise or audio artifacts. Psychic and mediumistic sessions are also viewed with skepticism due to the subjective nature of these interactions.

Some researchers attempt to integrate scientific and supernatural explanations, acknowledging that the human mind and experience are complex. They recognize that while some paranormal claims may be explained by natural phenomena or psychological factors, others remain unexplained and intriguing.

The evidence and theories put forth by researchers and paranormal experts regarding the Catacombs of Paris vary widely, reflecting the complexity of the human experience and our fascination with the unknown. As investigators and enthusiasts explore the catacombs, they contribute to an ongoing dialogue that merges history, science, and the supernatural.

While scientific investigations provide tangible evidence of the catacombs' historical significance and their place in Parisian history, paranormal claims offer a subjective and experiential perspective that draws people into the realm of wonder and mystery.

Ultimately, the Catacombs of Paris continue to captivate our imagination, reminding us of the enigmatic nature of the human experience and the enduring allure of the past and the unseen.

The discrepancies between scientific investigations and paranormal claims regarding the Catacombs of Paris highlight the importance of critical thinking and open-mindedness. Rather than viewing these perspectives as mutually exclusive, there is value in acknowledging and exploring the nuances that lie within the complex tapestry of human understanding.

One way to bridge the gap between scientific and paranormal perspectives is to encourage interdisciplinary collaboration. By bringing together experts from various fields, such as historians, archaeologists, anthropologists, geologists, psychologists, and paranormal investigators, a more comprehensive understanding of the catacombs can be achieved.

This collaborative approach allows for a diverse range of insights and interpretations, fostering an environment where empirical evidence and subjective experiences are considered equally valuable.

Both scientific investigations and paranormal inquiries benefit from rigorous methodology and research standards. Scientific studies must follow established protocols to ensure reliability and validity, while paranormal investigations should aim for transparency and thorough documentation of experiences and evidence.

By adhering to robust methodologies, researchers and investigators can build stronger cases for their respective claims and allow for more meaningful debates and discussions.

The human mind is a powerful tool that can influence how individuals perceive and interpret their surroundings. The psychological aspect of paranormal experiences is an essential consideration in understanding such phenomena.

Researchers can explore the power of suggestion, cognitive biases, and the role of cultural beliefs in shaping paranormal claims. Understanding how our minds process and interpret experiences can lead to a deeper appreciation of the human capacity for wonder and fascination.

The Catacombs of Paris hold historical, cultural, and spiritual significance. When conducting investigations, researchers and paranormal experts alike should approach the site with respect for its past and the individuals laid to rest there.

SECRETS OF THE BONE LABYRINTH: THE HAUNTED CATACOMBS OF PARIS

Responsible inquiry involves acknowledging the sanctity of the catacombs, preserving its integrity, and maintaining ethical practices during investigations.

The Catacombs of Paris, with their rich history and enigmatic atmosphere, invite us to embrace ambiguity. It is essential to recognize that not every question will have a definitive answer and that some mysteries may remain unsolved.

This embrace of ambiguity fosters humility and encourages a sense of awe and curiosity about the world around us.

The exploration of the Catacombs of Paris encompasses both scientific and supernatural dimensions, each contributing to the tapestry of human knowledge and understanding. Embracing the diversity of perspectives allows us to embark on a journey of discovery that transcends the boundaries of traditional disciplines.

As researchers and paranormal experts delve into the depths of the Bone Labyrinth, they offer us glimpses into the complexities of our history, our beliefs, and our shared fascination with the unknown. The Catacombs continue to be a place of wonder, where the past and the present converge, inviting us to ponder the mysteries that lie beneath the bustling streets of Paris. Whether through empirical evidence or personal experience, the Catacombs remind us that the pursuit of knowledge and the appreciation of the mysterious are timeless and interconnected aspects of the human spirit.

EDWARD TURNER

Chapter 9: The Dark Arts and Occult

The historical ties between the Catacombs of Paris and occult practices add an intriguing layer of mystique to this underground realm. Over the centuries, the catacombs have been associated with various esoteric and occult beliefs, drawing the interest of practitioners and seekers of the supernatural.

During the 19th century, Paris experienced a revival of occultism, with esoteric societies and secret orders gaining popularity. The catacombs, with their dark and mysterious atmosphere, captured the imagination of occultists, who saw the underground realm as a potent setting for their rituals and ceremonies.

Occult practitioners and spiritualists were drawn to the catacombs for conducting rituals, séances, and other mystical practices. These ceremonies often aimed to contact the spirits of the deceased or tap into the spiritual energies believed to permeate the underground space.

For some occultists, the catacombs represented a place of hidden knowledge and ancient wisdom. The labyrinthine passages were seen as a metaphor for the journey of self-discovery and spiritual enlightenment. Exploring the catacombs became an endeavor to unlock hidden truths and esoteric insights.

The catacombs, as a repository of human bones and relics, held powerful symbolism related to death and rebirth. Occultists often interpreted the underground realm as a gateway between the world of the living and the realm of the dead, reflecting the cyclical nature of life and the journey of the soul.

Over time, legends and folklore surrounding the catacombs took on occult elements. Stories of ghostly apparitions, mysterious energies, and supernatural encounters added to the perception of the catacombs as a place where the veil between worlds was thin.

The catacombs' association with death and transformation resonated with the principles of alchemy, an ancient mystical practice focused on spiritual enlightenment and the transmutation of base substances into gold. Occultists saw parallels between the alchemical processes and the catacombs' role as a place of transformation and spiritual metamorphosis.

Occultists sometimes interpreted historical events associated with the catacombs through esoteric lenses. For example, the French Revolution and the use of the catacombs as a place of refuge for revolutionaries were seen as symbolic of a larger cosmic struggle between light and darkness.

The catacombs' allure also permeated literature and art of the period. Authors and artists often drew inspiration from the catacombs' eerie ambiance and occult associations, incorporating them into their works to evoke themes of mystery, death, and the supernatural.

SECRETS OF THE BONE LABYRINTH: THE HAUNTED CATACOMBS OF PARIS

The historical ties between the Catacombs of Paris and occult practices illustrate the enduring fascination with the mysteries of life and death. The underground realm served as a canvas for occultists and seekers of hidden knowledge, who saw in its dark passages a reflection of their esoteric beliefs and spiritual quests.

While the catacombs' occult associations add to its allure, they also underscore the complexity of human beliefs and our perpetual fascination with the unknown. The occult undercurrents of the Catacombs continue to capture our imagination, inviting us to explore the interplay between history, spirituality, and the mysterious forces that shape our perception of the world.

Modern Occult Interest and Practices:

Even in contemporary times, the catacombs maintain their allure within the occult community. Occult enthusiasts, spiritual seekers, and practitioners of various esoteric traditions are drawn to the catacombs' enigmatic atmosphere and historical significance. Some modern practices and interests include:

1. Occult Tours and Events: The catacombs have become a popular destination for occult-themed tours and events. Occultists and enthusiasts participate in guided tours that blend historical facts with stories of supernatural encounters and mysterious legends.

2. Rituals and Ceremonies: Occult practitioners occasionally conduct rituals and ceremonies within the catacombs. These

practices might draw inspiration from various traditions, such as Wicca, modern witchcraft, and ceremonial magic, seeking to harness the energy of the underground realm for spiritual purposes.

3. Ghost Hunts and Paranormal Investigations: Paranormal investigators and ghost hunters continue to explore the catacombs in search of supernatural phenomena. They employ sophisticated equipment and recording devices to capture potential evidence of ghostly activity and paranormal occurrences.

4. Occult Art and Literature: The catacombs' haunting ambiance inspires contemporary artists, writers, and musicians to incorporate occult themes into their works. Paintings, literature, and music often draw upon the catacombs' symbolism and atmosphere to evoke a sense of mystery and spiritual exploration.

5. Esoteric Interpretations: Modern occultists still interpret the catacombs through esoteric lenses, viewing them as sacred sites of hidden wisdom and mystical significance. Some believe that the catacombs hold ancient secrets waiting to be revealed through spiritual practices and intuitive insights.

6. An Embrace of Mystery: For many within the occult community, the catacombs represent a place where the boundaries between the mundane and the magical blur. The allure of the unknown and the mysteries that lie beneath the surface continue to captivate individuals seeking spiritual growth and enlightenment.

SECRETS OF THE BONE LABYRINTH: THE HAUNTED CATACOMBS OF PARIS

While modern occult interests in the catacombs add to the realm's enigmatic reputation, it is essential to emphasize the importance of respecting the cultural heritage and historical significance of this sacred site. Practitioners and enthusiasts should approach the catacombs with reverence, understanding that it is a place of solemn remembrance for the millions of souls laid to rest there.

Engaging in occult practices within the catacombs should be done responsibly, adhering to ethical guidelines and showing respect for the site's historical context. Balancing the pursuit of esoteric exploration with a sense of reverence for the past ensures that the catacombs remain a place of wonder and contemplation for generations to come.

The historical ties between the Catacombs of Paris and occult practices have woven a rich tapestry of mystery and fascination. From the 19th-century occult revival to modern-day interests, the catacombs continue to be a place that evokes a sense of wonder and spiritual exploration.

While some may view the catacombs' occult associations as speculative or subjective, they contribute to the enduring allure of this underground realm. The catacombs remain a place of intrigue, inviting individuals to contemplate the mysteries of life and death, the interconnectedness of history and spirituality, and the profound quest for hidden knowledge that transcends time and place.

The Catacombs of Paris have long been associated with secret societies and clandestine rituals, adding an air of intrigue and mystery to their historical significance. While concrete evidence of these activities is often scarce, historical accounts and legends suggest that secret societies and rituals did indeed thrive within the underground labyrinth.

During the French Revolution, the Catacombs of Paris became a refuge for secret societies, one of which was known as the Cult of the Innocents. This group held esoteric beliefs and sought to find hidden knowledge and spiritual enlightenment within the catacombs' depths.

The Cult of the Innocents was known for conducting mysterious rituals and ceremonies, often involving candles, incense, and chanting. They believed that the catacombs held ancient secrets and that by connecting with the spirits of the deceased, they could gain wisdom and guidance.

Another secret society rumored to have frequented the catacombs during the 18th century was the Philadelphes. This group was influenced by Freemasonry and practiced a blend of mystical and alchemical traditions.

The Philadelphes held meetings and rituals within the catacombs, where they believed they could commune with the spirits of the dead and tap into hidden spiritual energies. They saw the catacombs as a place of transformation and sought to gain insight into the mysteries of life and death.

The Cataflics, the mysterious guardians of the catacombs, were believed to be more than just police officers tasked with deterring trespassers. Legends suggested that the Cataflics were initiated into ancient rituals and secret knowledge that had been passed down through generations.

It was said that the Cataflics guarded not only the physical safety of the catacombs but also the spiritual secrets and hidden wisdom believed to reside within. These guardians were said to possess esoteric knowledge and an understanding of the catacombs' deeper mysteries.

Over the centuries, there have been reports of occult gatherings and ceremonies taking place within the catacombs. Occultists and secret societies saw the underground realm as an ideal setting for their esoteric practices, where they could tap into the energies of the dead and the spiritual forces they believed were present.

These gatherings often involved rituals, symbolism, and the use of sacred objects. The catacombs' dark and mysterious atmosphere lent itself to the sense of secrecy and reverence that these groups sought.

Legends surrounding the catacombs tell of hidden chambers and artifacts that hold ancient wisdom and mystical power. Some believe that certain secret societies left behind clues and symbols within the catacombs that lead to these hidden spaces.

These legends fuel the imaginations of seekers and adventurers who are drawn to the catacombs in search of the unknown and the mysterious.

While much of the historical evidence concerning secret societies and rituals within the Catacombs of Paris remains elusive, the stories and legends that persist add to the realm's enigmatic allure. The catacombs' dark and labyrinthine passages have fueled the imaginations of those seeking hidden knowledge and spiritual enlightenment.

Whether these stories are based on historical facts or the products of myths and legends, they contribute to the mystique of the catacombs and serve as a reminder of the shadows of the past that continue to captivate our curiosity and fascination. The Catacombs of Paris remain a place where the historical and the mystical converge, inviting us to explore the depths of human history and the enduring quest for secrets and wisdom hidden within the underground labyrinth.

The legacy of secret societies and rituals within the Catacombs of Paris has left an indelible mark on its history and cultural significance. Even in the absence of concrete evidence, the stories and legends surrounding these clandestine activities continue to intrigue historians, occultists, and visitors alike.

The tales of secret societies and rituals within the catacombs have inspired numerous works of art and literature. Authors, poets, and artists have drawn upon the catacombs' mystical associations to create stories of intrigue, mystery, and supernatural encounters.

From Gothic novels to dark-themed artworks, the catacombs' enigmatic reputation has served as a backdrop for tales of hidden societies, forbidden knowledge, and esoteric rituals.

The catacombs' historical ties to the occult have contributed to the site's legacy as a place of fascination for modern occultists and esoteric practitioners. For those who follow mystical traditions and seek spiritual enlightenment, the catacombs hold an aura of mystery and spiritual significance.

Occultists continue to be drawn to the catacombs, seeking to connect with its hidden energies and tap into the esoteric knowledge they believe lies beneath the surface.

The association of the catacombs with secret societies and occult practices has also impacted tourism and cultural interest in the site. Occult-themed tours and events attract visitors eager to explore the catacombs' mysterious past and immerse themselves in its haunting atmosphere.

The catacombs' reputation as a place of hidden knowledge and spiritual significance adds to its allure as a cultural landmark, drawing tourists and enthusiasts from around the world.

Whether the stories of secret societies and rituals within the catacombs are grounded in historical reality or embellished by legend, they contribute to the sense of wonder and speculation that surrounds this underground realm.

The catacombs remain a place where history, myth, and the supernatural intersect, inviting contemplation and curiosity about the mysteries that lie hidden beneath the bustling streets of Paris.

The legacy of secret societies and rituals within the Catacombs of Paris serves as a testament to the power of human imagination. Throughout history, people have been captivated by tales of hidden knowledge, mystical practices, and the quest for the unknown.

The catacombs embody the human fascination with the enigmatic and the desire to explore the depths of existence beyond the mundane.

While the historical ties between the Catacombs of Paris and secret societies may be obscured by the passage of time, the veil of mystery surrounding this underground labyrinth endures. The stories of occult practices and esoteric gatherings within the catacombs continue to fuel the imaginations of those who seek the unknown and the mystical.

As visitors explore the dark passages and bone-lined chambers, they become part of a centuries-old tradition of fascination with the Catacombs of Paris. This underground realm remains a place where history and legend intertwine, and where the allure of the mysterious and the esoteric beckons those who dare to venture into the depths of the Bone Labyrinth.

SECRETS OF THE BONE LABYRINTH: THE HAUNTED CATACOMBS OF PARIS

Chapter 10: Echoes of the Past

The Catacombs of Paris are adorned with numerous inscriptions, graffiti, and symbols left behind by various visitors over the centuries. Decoding these hidden messages and symbols can be challenging, as many are cryptic or have been worn away by time and environmental factors. However, some recurring themes and common elements have been identified:

1. Names and Dates:

Many inscriptions in the Catacombs consist of names and dates, left by visitors as a way to mark their presence and commemorate their exploration. These inscriptions may also include messages of remembrance or expressions of awe and wonder at the catacombs' unique ambiance.

2. Spiritual and Occult Symbols:

As a site with historical ties to the occult, some symbols found within the catacombs have esoteric significance. These may include pentagrams, crosses, and other mystical symbols associated with secret societies and mystical practices.

3. Poetic and Philosophical Verses:

Some inscriptions take the form of poetic or philosophical verses, reflecting on themes such as mortality, the passage of time, and the human condition. These inscriptions often add to the catacombs' aura of contemplation and reflection.

4. Symbols of Death and Rebirth:

Given the catacombs' function as an ossuary, symbols of death and rebirth are prevalent. These may include images of skulls, skeletons, and other macabre motifs. For some, these symbols represent the cyclical nature of life and the transformative power of death.

5. Historical Graffiti:

Over the centuries, the catacombs have been visited by a diverse array of people, from tourists to soldiers during times of war. Some inscriptions are historical graffiti, providing glimpses into the experiences and emotions of those who have explored the catacombs throughout history.

6. Messages of Defiance and Rebellion:

During times of political turmoil, the catacombs served as a refuge for those seeking shelter from authorities. Some inscriptions and graffiti may contain messages of defiance, rebellion, or political statements.

7. Cryptic Symbols and Markings:

Not all inscriptions within the catacombs are immediately decipherable. Some symbols and markings may have personal or symbolic meaning for the individual who left them, while others could be remnants of secret societies or coded messages.

8. The Quest for Hidden Knowledge:

Occultists and seekers of hidden knowledge may have left inscriptions that reference esoteric teachings, mystical experiences, or their quest for spiritual enlightenment.

Decoding the hidden messages and inscriptions found within the Catacombs of Paris can be an intricate task. Some inscriptions may be clear and easily understood, while others remain cryptic and open to interpretation.

Historians, archaeologists, and enthusiasts continue to study these inscriptions in an effort to understand their significance and context within the catacombs' history. Additionally, technology and conservation efforts are used to preserve and document these inscriptions, ensuring that their hidden messages can be studied and appreciated by future generations.

Decoding and understanding the hidden messages and inscriptions within the Catacombs of Paris is not only an intellectual pursuit but also an essential aspect of preserving the site's cultural heritage. Each inscription serves as a unique window into the past, shedding light on the people, beliefs, and emotions of those who once traversed these underground passages.

Efforts are underway to document and catalog the inscriptions to ensure their preservation and interpretation. Advanced imaging techniques, such as laser scanning and high-resolution photography, are used to capture the intricate details of the inscriptions without causing any damage to the delicate environment.

Decoding the hidden messages within the catacombs requires an interdisciplinary approach that involves historians, archaeologists, linguists, art conservators, and specialists in occult studies. Collaboration between these experts helps to gain a comprehensive understanding of the inscriptions, drawing on various fields of knowledge.

Context plays a crucial role in decoding the inscriptions. Studying the location, positioning, and content of each inscription can provide valuable clues about the intent and motivations of those who left them behind.

Inscriptions near religious symbols or graves may indicate spiritual reverence, while inscriptions in areas frequented by secret societies could reveal their presence. Historical graffiti left during significant events, such as wars or revolutions, can offer insight into the emotions and perspectives of the people living during those times.

While deciphering the inscriptions offers valuable historical insights, preserving some level of mystery is also important. The catacombs' aura of enigma is part of what makes them an alluring and captivating site. Leaving some inscriptions and symbols shrouded in mystery allows future generations to continue pondering and interpreting the hidden messages within these ancient walls.

As visitors continue to explore the Catacombs of Paris, it is crucial to practice responsible visitation. Vandalism and unnecessary touching of the inscriptions can cause irreparable damage to these delicate historical artifacts. Visitors are encouraged to observe and appreciate the inscriptions without altering or defacing them in any way.

Decoding the hidden messages and inscriptions found within the Catacombs of Paris is an ongoing and captivating endeavor. Each inscription tells a unique story of the past, providing glimpses into the lives, beliefs, and emotions of those who have wandered through the underground labyrinth.

As historians and specialists continue their research and conservation efforts, the catacombs' hidden messages will continue to be unraveled, adding to the rich tapestry of human history and the enduring allure of this remarkable underground realm. The Catacombs of Paris stand as a testament to the timeless desire to leave our mark on the world and to explore the depths of existence, both in life and in the mysteries that lie beyond the threshold of mortality.

Unraveling the significance of the markings and inscriptions within the Catacombs of Paris requires careful examination of their context and historical events that might have influenced their creation. While some inscriptions are straightforward and directly related to historical events, others may carry symbolic or personal meanings. Here are some potential connections between the markings and historical events:

1. Revolutionary Era Graffiti:

During the French Revolution in the late 18th century, the catacombs served as a refuge for revolutionaries and secret societies. Graffiti and inscriptions from this period may contain political messages, revolutionary slogans, or symbols of defiance against the monarchy.

Decoding these markings can provide insights into the sentiments and aspirations of the people who sought shelter in the catacombs during this tumultuous time in French history.

2. Commemorating Battles and Wars:

As a site of historical importance, the catacombs may have witnessed various battles and conflicts. Inscriptions and symbols related to military events could indicate memorialization or acts of remembrance for fallen soldiers.

For example, during World War II, the catacombs were used as a hideout and headquarters by the French Resistance. Graffiti and inscriptions from this period might reflect the struggle for liberation and the courage of those who fought against the Nazi occupation.

3. Esoteric Symbolism and Occult Beliefs:

Given the catacombs' association with occult practices and secret societies, some inscriptions may be laden with esoteric symbolism and mysticism. Occultists and spiritual seekers may have left markings that convey their quest for hidden knowledge, spiritual enlightenment, or their belief in mystical forces within the underground realm.

4. Pilgrimages and Religious Visits:

Throughout history, the catacombs have attracted religious pilgrims seeking a connection with the deceased and the divine. Inscriptions and symbols left by religious visitors may reflect acts of devotion, prayers for the souls of the departed, or expressions of religious significance tied to historical events or religious festivals.

5. Historical Significance of Names and Dates:

Many inscriptions simply bear names and dates, which may serve as records of past visitors or significant events. These markings may be left by individuals who sought to leave their mark on the catacombs or commemorate their visit during important moments in their lives.

6. Personal Journals and Emotional Outpourings:

Some inscriptions may act as personal journals, providing glimpses into the emotions and experiences of those who explored the catacombs. These writings might include expressions of wonder, fear, awe, or reflections on mortality and the passage of time.

7. Connections to Urban Exploration and Modern History:

In recent times, urban explorers have left their own marks in the catacombs. Graffiti and inscriptions from the modern era may represent contemporary cultural trends, political statements, or reflections on the catacombs' enduring fascination.

The significance of the markings and inscriptions within the Catacombs of Paris is multifaceted, reflecting the layers of history that have shaped this underground realm. Each inscription tells a unique story, connecting the catacombs to historical events, personal experiences, and enduring human beliefs and emotions.

By carefully examining the context and historical background of these markings, researchers can piece together the historical narrative of the catacombs and the diverse individuals who have contributed to its rich tapestry of human history. Unraveling the significance of these inscriptions provides us with a deeper understanding of the catacombs' cultural heritage and its enduring allure for generations past and present.

As historians, archaeologists, and enthusiasts continue to study and decode the markings within the Catacombs of Paris, they uncover hidden narratives that enhance our understanding of the past. Each inscription represents a fragment of history, and together, they create a mosaic of human experiences and emotions throughout the ages.

Decoding the markings within the catacombs allows us to hear the voices of those who came before us. From the revolutionaries seeking refuge during times of political upheaval to the spiritual pilgrims seeking solace and connection, each inscription provides a personal insight into the lives of individuals who have walked these ancient corridors.

The markings and inscriptions bridge the gap between the distant past and the present, forging a human connection across time. They remind us that, regardless of the era, people have sought meaning, solace, and expression within the catacombs.

Many inscriptions within the catacombs reflect on mortality and the transient nature of human existence. They serve as poignant reminders of our mortality, inspiring us to contemplate the brevity of life and the timeless quest for understanding the mysteries of death.

Graffiti and inscriptions from periods of political unrest provide a glimpse into the thoughts and sentiments of those living through tumultuous times. They offer commentary on social and political issues, often expressing hopes for change, calls for justice, or defiance against oppressive regimes.

The occult symbols and esoteric markings within the catacombs speak to a deep yearning for hidden knowledge and spiritual enlightenment. They represent a tradition of seeking meaning beyond the surface of existence, tapping into the ancient mysteries that have captivated human minds throughout history.

The process of decoding and studying these markings is essential for preserving the cultural heritage of the catacombs. As visitors and researchers explore these underground passageways, they must do so with care and respect to ensure that these historical inscriptions endure for future generations.

The significance of the markings within the catacombs extends beyond the historical events they may be connected to. As contemporary visitors leave their own marks and inscriptions, they become part of an ongoing narrative, contributing to the ever-evolving history of this unique and sacred site.

The markings and inscriptions within the Catacombs of Paris form a living tapestry of time, weaving together the stories of countless individuals who have ventured into the depths of this subterranean realm. Decoding their hidden messages and uncovering their historical connections not only enriches our understanding of the past but also adds to the mystique and allure of the catacombs for present and future generations.

As we continue to explore the catacombs, we are reminded of the shared human experiences that transcend time and connect us to those who have walked these underground passages before us. The catacombs stand as a powerful symbol of the enduring human quest for meaning, the contemplation of mortality, and the fascination with the unknown, encapsulated in the hidden narratives etched upon its walls.

SECRETS OF THE BONE LABYRINTH: THE HAUNTED CATACOMBS OF PARIS

Chapter 11: Catacombs Exploration Culture

───

I n recent years, the Catacombs of Paris have witnessed a growing trend in urban exploration. Urban exploration, often referred to as "urbex," involves exploring and photographing abandoned or off-limits urban areas, including historical sites, industrial facilities, and underground locations like the catacombs.

The Catacombs of Paris, with their underground maze of tunnels and historical significance, have become an attractive destination for urban explorers seeking adventure, mystery, and unique photographic opportunities. The trend has been fueled by social media platforms and online forums where urbex enthusiasts share their experiences and photos, inspiring others to embark on similar expeditions.

While urban exploration in the Catacombs of Paris offers an alluring sense of adventure and discovery, it is essential to recognize the associated risks and potential dangers:

1. Legal Consequences:

Urban exploration often involves trespassing into off-limits or restricted areas, including historical monuments like the catacombs. Unauthorized entry into such sites can lead to legal consequences, including fines and possible criminal charges.

2. Physical Hazards:

The catacombs pose numerous physical hazards to urban explorers. The underground passages are dark, narrow, and uneven, making it easy to trip or get lost. Sections of the catacombs may be unstable or prone to collapse, putting explorers at risk of injury or entrapment.

3. Psychological Impact:

Navigating the catacombs' labyrinthine passages can be disorienting and mentally challenging, particularly for those without prior experience in underground exploration. The eerie and claustrophobic environment may lead to feelings of anxiety, stress, or panic.

4. Risk of Getting Lost:

The Catacombs of Paris cover an extensive area with numerous interconnected passages. Without proper navigation skills or equipment, explorers may get lost and find it difficult to retrace their steps to the exit.

5. Encountering the Unknown:

During urban exploration, explorers may encounter unexpected hazards or wildlife within the catacombs. Additionally, they might come across other people, such as vandals, squatters, or individuals engaging in illegal activities, which could lead to confrontations.

6. Preservation Concerns:

SECRETS OF THE BONE LABYRINTH: THE HAUNTED CATACOMBS OF PARIS

Increased foot traffic from urban exploration can cause additional wear and tear on the delicate catacombs, potentially leading to damage to historical artifacts, inscriptions, and the overall structural integrity of the site.

To mitigate the risks associated with urban exploration in the Catacombs of Paris, it is crucial to promote responsible exploration practices:

- Obtain Permissions: Urban explorers should seek appropriate permissions and access to explore the catacombs legally, respecting the rules and regulations set by the authorities.

- Safety Precautions: Explorers should be well-prepared and equipped with proper safety gear, including sturdy footwear, headlamps, maps, and navigation tools. It is advisable to explore with a group, as well as inform someone outside the catacombs of the planned expedition.

- Preserve and Protect: Urban explorers should be mindful of preserving the historical and cultural heritage of the catacombs. Avoid touching, defacing, or removing any artifacts or inscriptions, and refrain from leaving behind any trash or litter.

- Know Your Limits: It is essential for explorers to understand their own physical and psychological limits before embarking on such expeditions. Proper training and experience in urban exploration can help ensure safer and more enjoyable adventures.

The growing trend of urban exploration in the Catacombs of Paris offers adventurous souls a chance to delve into the mysteries of the underground realm. However, it is vital to balance the excitement of exploration with responsible and mindful practices to protect both personal safety and the cultural significance of this historical site.

By promoting responsible exploration and understanding the potential risks, urban explorers can continue to enjoy the thrill of discovering the hidden wonders of the Catacombs of Paris while respecting the historical legacy and preserving this unique heritage for generations to come.

Promoting responsible exploration involves collaboration between urban explorers and the authorities responsible for the preservation and management of the Catacombs of Paris. By engaging in open dialogue, explorers can gain valuable insights into the site's history, potential hazards, and guidelines for responsible exploration.

Authorities, in turn, can better understand the motivations and interests of urban explorers and work together to create a balance between preservation and access. This collaboration can lead to the establishment of guided tours or controlled access periods, allowing enthusiasts to experience the catacombs' mystique while minimizing negative impacts on the site.

Education plays a crucial role in promoting responsible urban exploration. Online communities and organizations focused on urban exploration can emphasize the importance of safety, respect for historical sites, and adherence to local laws and regulations.

Experienced explorers can share tips and best practices to help newcomers navigate the catacombs safely. Emphasizing the potential risks and the need for preparation can encourage individuals to approach urban exploration with caution and responsibility.

Beyond responsible exploration practices, active preservation efforts are vital to safeguarding the catacombs' historical and cultural heritage. Collaborative efforts between government agencies, preservation organizations, and the public can work to maintain the catacombs' structural integrity and protect its unique artifacts and inscriptions.

Funding raised through guided tours or donations could be dedicated to preservation projects aimed at restoring damaged areas and maintaining the catacombs for future generations of explorers and visitors.

Promoting a strong sense of community and ethical exploration within the urban exploration community can foster a culture of responsible practices. Encouraging explorers to respect the sites they visit and to leave no trace behind can help preserve the integrity of the catacombs and other urban exploration destinations.

The urban exploration community can also actively engage in cleanup and restoration initiatives, contributing to the conservation of these historical landmarks.

Responsible exploration seeks to strike a balance between adventure and preservation, recognizing that historical sites like the Catacombs of Paris are irreplaceable cultural treasures. By approaching exploration with sensitivity and respect for the site's historical value, enthusiasts can continue to enjoy the allure of the catacombs while safeguarding its heritage for generations to come.

Responsible urban exploration transforms adventurers into stewards, ensuring that the Catacombs of Paris remain accessible and protected, allowing visitors to be captivated by its mysteries while preserving the site's cultural and historical significance.

The growing trend of urban exploration in the Catacombs of Paris presents both opportunities and challenges. Responsible exploration practices, collaboration with authorities, preservation efforts, and ethical values within the urban exploration community all play critical roles in maintaining the integrity of this historical site.

Urban explorers, as modern-day adventurers, have the power to protect and preserve the past while embracing the excitement of uncovering hidden treasures. By fostering a culture of responsible exploration, enthusiasts can ensure that the Catacombs of Paris continue to be a captivating destination for future generations, where the allure of history and adventure intertwine in the shadowy depths of the Bone Labyrinth.

SECRETS OF THE BONE LABYRINTH: THE HAUNTED CATACOMBS OF PARIS

The community of adventurers and enthusiasts who seek to document the enigmatic world of the Catacombs of Paris is a diverse and passionate group. United by their fascination with historical exploration and the mysteries of the underground, these individuals come from various backgrounds, including urban exploration, history, photography, archaeology, and the paranormal.

Urban explorers, often referred to as "urbexers," form a significant part of the community. These individuals are driven by a curiosity to discover and document hidden and abandoned places, including the catacombs. They are attracted to the catacombs' rich history, its intricate network of tunnels, and the opportunity to capture unique and atmospheric photographs.

Historians and archaeologists are drawn to the catacombs as well, seeking to unravel its historical significance and decode the inscriptions and symbols left by past generations. They contribute their expertise in historical research and preservation, helping to contextualize the catacombs within the broader history of Paris and Europe.

The catacombs' haunting ambiance and dramatic visuals inspire photographers and media enthusiasts. Armed with cameras and often accompanied by lighting equipment, they aim to capture the subterranean world in all its eerie splendor. Their work helps bring the catacombs to life for audiences around the world.

For some, the catacombs' reputation for ghostly encounters and eerie tales is a compelling draw. Paranormal investigators and enthusiasts explore the catacombs in search of supernatural phenomena and attempt to document any potential evidence of ghostly activity.

The catacombs' rich history and enigmatic atmosphere make it a captivating setting for filmmakers and storytellers. Documentaries, short films, and written accounts centering around the catacombs are created to share the site's history and intrigue with wider audiences.

Amidst the enthusiasm for exploration, there are those within the community who advocate for the preservation and responsible documentation of the catacombs. They emphasize the need to protect the site's cultural and historical heritage and educate others about the importance of sustainable exploration.

The digital age has connected catacomb enthusiasts from around the world. Online communities and forums dedicated to urban exploration and historical sites provide platforms for sharing experiences, photographs, and research. These platforms foster a sense of camaraderie and allow enthusiasts to learn from one another.

The community of catacomb enthusiasts often collaborates on research projects, exploration expeditions, and documentation efforts. They share knowledge, insights, and discoveries, enriching each other's understanding of the catacombs' hidden world.

SECRETS OF THE BONE LABYRINTH: THE HAUNTED CATACOMBS OF PARIS

The community of adventurers and enthusiasts who seek to document the Catacombs of Paris is united by their fascination with the enigmatic world hidden beneath the streets of the city. Their diverse skills, passions, and perspectives contribute to a holistic exploration of this historical site, illuminating its mysteries and preserving its cultural legacy.

As they navigate the underground labyrinth, these individuals are captivated by the echoes of the past, the ethereal atmosphere, and the enduring allure of the Catacombs of Paris. Through their collective efforts, they continue to unravel the hidden narratives etched within the catacombs' walls, preserving its secrets and sharing its wonders with the world beyond.

Within the community of catacomb enthusiasts, collaborative exploration projects are common. These projects bring together individuals with different expertise, from historians and archaeologists to urban explorers and photographers. Working as a team, they embark on well-planned expeditions to explore and document different sections of the catacombs.

Collaborative projects allow for a more comprehensive understanding of the catacombs' history, architecture, and hidden mysteries. They also provide an opportunity to pool resources, share knowledge, and ensure safety during exploration.

Enthusiasts within the catacomb community are committed to preserving the knowledge they gain from their explorations. They actively contribute to archives, academic papers, and historical databases, ensuring that their findings are accessible to researchers, historians, and the public.

By sharing their discoveries, the community contributes to the collective understanding of the catacombs and enhances the cultural appreciation of this historical site.

The catacombs' underground world remains largely unseen by the public. Catacomb enthusiasts seek to change that by documenting their experiences through photography, videos, and written accounts.

Their work showcases the catacombs' haunting beauty, historical inscriptions, and the eerie atmosphere that permeates the underground passageways. Through these creative expressions, enthusiasts invite others to share in the wonder and enigma of the catacombs.

A significant aspect of the catacomb community's role is advocating for the preservation of historical sites and responsible exploration practices. Enthusiasts strive to raise awareness about the importance of conserving the catacombs and other historical landmarks, emphasizing the need to protect them for future generations.

Advocacy also includes promoting responsible behavior during exploration, respecting the site's cultural significance, and adhering to legal regulations.

The catacomb community's dedication to documenting and sharing the secrets of the underground realm helps inspire cultural appreciation and interest in history. Their efforts contribute to fostering a deeper connection between people and historical sites, encouraging respect for the past and a sense of stewardship for the future.

The community of catacomb enthusiasts serves as a source of inspiration for future generations of explorers, historians, and preservationists. Their passion for unraveling historical mysteries and exploring hidden worlds encourages others to engage with history and cultural heritage in new and exciting ways.

By nurturing a sense of wonder and curiosity, the catacomb community ensures that the allure of historical exploration will continue to thrive for years to come.

The community of adventurers and enthusiasts who seek to document the Catacombs of Paris can be considered guardians of an enigmatic legacy. Through their collective efforts, they unlock the secrets of the underground realm, preserve its cultural heritage, and share its captivating wonders with the world.

Their dedication to responsible exploration, historical research, and advocacy for preservation ensures that the catacombs remain a site of cultural significance, captivating the imaginations of generations to come. United by their passion for history, exploration, and cultural appreciation, these enthusiasts form a unique community that reveres the past, cherishes the present, and safeguards an enigmatic world hidden beneath the heart of Paris.

EDWARD TURNER

Chapter 12: Navigating the Forbidden

E ntering the Catacombs of Paris without permission is considered trespassing and can lead to significant legal consequences. The catacombs are a protected historical site, and access to certain areas is strictly controlled to preserve their cultural and historical significance.

1. Trespassing Laws:

Trespassing is a criminal offense in most jurisdictions, including France, where the Catacombs of Paris are located. Unauthorized entry into the catacombs can result in criminal charges, which may include fines, imprisonment, or both, depending on the severity of the violation and local laws.

2. Damage to Property:

Entering the catacombs without permission can lead to damage to historical artifacts, inscriptions, or the structure of the catacombs themselves. Any intentional or unintentional damage caused during the trespassing can lead to additional charges related to vandalism or destruction of property.

3. Rescue Costs:

If trespassers become lost or injured within the catacombs and require rescue or assistance from emergency services, they may be held financially responsible for the costs incurred during the rescue operation.

4. Civil Liability:

Trespassers may also face civil liability if their actions cause harm to others or result in damages to private property adjacent to the catacombs.

5. Increased Surveillance and Enforcement:

The increasing popularity of urban exploration in the catacombs has prompted authorities to implement more stringent security measures to deter unauthorized access. These measures may include enhanced surveillance, increased patrols, and monitoring of entry points.

6. Criminal Records and Travel Restrictions:

Convictions for trespassing can result in criminal records, which may have long-term consequences for individuals' personal and professional lives. Additionally, some countries may deny entry to individuals with criminal records, which could impact international travel plans.

7. Respect for Cultural Heritage:

Beyond legal consequences, unauthorized entry into the catacombs undermines efforts to preserve and protect cultural heritage sites. It demonstrates a lack of respect for the historical significance of the catacombs and the efforts made by preservationists and authorities to maintain its integrity.

SECRETS OF THE BONE LABYRINTH: THE HAUNTED CATACOMBS OF PARIS

The legal aspects and consequences of entering the Catacombs of Paris without permission are clear and should be heeded by all. Trespassing not only carries legal ramifications but also risks damaging the delicate historical site and its inscriptions, which hold immense cultural and historical value.

Instead of engaging in unauthorized exploration, enthusiasts should respect the significance of the catacombs and appreciate them through legal and responsible means. Guided tours and authorized access points allow visitors to experience the mystique and allure of the Catacombs of Paris while ensuring the preservation of its enigmatic legacy for generations to come.

To avoid the legal consequences of trespassing, individuals interested in exploring the Catacombs of Paris should consider responsible and legal alternatives. There are authorized ways to experience the catacombs while respecting its cultural significance and adhering to the law:

1. Guided Tours:

Guided tours are the most accessible and legal way to explore the catacombs. Official tours led by knowledgeable guides offer a safe and informative experience, providing visitors with historical context and ensuring that they stay within permitted areas.

2. Educational Programs:

In some instances, educational programs or workshops may provide limited access to specific sections of the catacombs for research or learning purposes. Universities, cultural institutions, or preservation organizations may offer such programs.

3. Research Permits:

For historians, archaeologists, or academics interested in studying specific aspects of the catacombs, research permits can be sought from the relevant authorities. These permits grant authorized access for scholarly purposes, ensuring the preservation of the site.

4. Photography and Media Permits:

If documenting the catacombs for artistic or media purposes, individuals can seek permits from the appropriate authorities. These permits outline specific guidelines for photography or filming, safeguarding the site and its heritage.

5. Engage with Preservation Organizations:

By supporting preservation organizations dedicated to the conservation of the catacombs, enthusiasts can contribute to the site's protection and maintenance. These organizations may offer opportunities to engage in volunteer work, supporting responsible exploration efforts.

6. Follow Local Regulations:

Understanding and adhering to local laws and regulations concerning the catacombs is essential for any visitor. Familiarizing oneself with the rules set by the responsible authorities helps ensure compliance and prevents legal issues.

SECRETS OF THE BONE LABYRINTH: THE HAUNTED CATACOMBS OF PARIS

Beyond complying with the law, responsible exploration promotes cultural awareness and appreciation. Enthusiasts who embrace legal alternatives also demonstrate respect for the catacombs' historical significance, contributing to the preservation of its enigmatic legacy.

Members of the catacomb community can play a vital role in educating others about the legal and ethical aspects of exploration. Through online platforms, workshops, and public engagement, they can raise awareness about the importance of preserving historical sites and the consequences of trespassing.

Responsible exploration is not just about avoiding legal consequences; it is about safeguarding the catacombs for future generations. By choosing authorized access options and supporting preservation efforts, enthusiasts can preserve the enigmatic world of the Catacombs of Paris in a manner that respects its historical and cultural value.

Engaging with the catacombs through legal means ensures that the allure of this underground realm endures while fostering a sense of stewardship for this unique heritage. By cherishing the catacombs responsibly, explorers become custodians of its enigmatic legacy, ensuring that its mysteries remain preserved for generations to come.

Preserving the Catacombs of Paris and protecting its historical significance is a multifaceted endeavor involving various measures and stakeholders. Over the years, authorities and preservation organizations have implemented a range of strategies to ensure the site's integrity and cultural value:

1. Restricted Access and Guided Tours:

One of the primary measures taken to protect the Catacombs is the restriction of access to certain areas. Most of the catacombs are off-limits to the general public, and visitors can only explore designated sections through guided tours. These tours are led by knowledgeable guides who provide historical context, ensure visitor safety, and prevent unauthorized exploration.

2. Monitoring and Surveillance:

To deter trespassers and unauthorized exploration, the catacombs are subject to monitoring and surveillance. Security measures, such as cameras and increased patrols, are employed to detect and respond to any illegal entry or suspicious activities.

3. Conservation and Restoration Efforts:

Conservation and restoration efforts are essential in maintaining the catacombs' structural integrity and preserving its historical artifacts and inscriptions. Preservationists work diligently to repair damage caused by age, environmental factors, and human activity, ensuring the catacombs remain intact for future generations.

4. Educational and Research Initiatives:

Engaging in educational and research initiatives allows experts to gain a deeper understanding of the catacombs' historical significance. Archaeological excavations, historical research, and scientific studies contribute to a comprehensive knowledge of the site, which, in turn, informs preservation efforts.

5. Community Involvement and Advocacy:

Preservation organizations and concerned citizens play a vital role in advocating for the protection of the catacombs. Community involvement includes raising awareness about the site's cultural value, organizing cleanup events, and supporting conservation projects.

6. Regulation and Legislation:

Governments and local authorities have enacted legislation and regulations to safeguard the catacombs' historical significance. These laws address issues such as unauthorized access, vandalism, and damage to the site.

7. Public Awareness and Education:

Educating the public about the importance of preserving the catacombs is key to fostering a culture of respect for historical sites. Informational exhibits, signage, and educational programs help visitors understand the significance of the catacombs and the need for responsible exploration.

8. Sustainable Tourism Management:

Managing tourism sustainably is crucial to minimizing the impact of visitor activity on the catacombs. Implementing visitor limits, ensuring proper waste disposal, and enforcing guidelines for photography and filming help balance tourism with preservation goals.

9. Partnerships and Funding:

Collaborating with private organizations, academic institutions, and international bodies provides additional resources for catacombs' preservation. Partnerships can secure funding for conservation projects, research endeavors, and public outreach.

The Catacombs of Paris stand as a testament to centuries of history and culture, making their preservation of paramount importance. Through a combination of restricted access, conservation efforts, community involvement, and public awareness, stakeholders work together to protect this enigmatic world beneath the bustling city.

By ensuring that future generations can experience the catacombs' allure, while respecting its historical significance, these measures help preserve the catacombs as a living legacy, offering visitors a glimpse into the mysteries of the past and safeguarding its cultural heritage for years to come.

Advancements in technology have played a significant role in preserving the Catacombs of Paris. Non-invasive techniques, such as 3D laser scanning and photogrammetry, allow experts to create detailed digital replicas of the catacombs' interiors. These digital models aid in documentation, research, and planning conservation efforts without physically disturbing the site.

Monitoring the catacombs' environmental conditions is crucial for preservation. Temperature, humidity, and air quality sensors are strategically placed to assess the impact of human activity and external factors on the catacombs' stability and artifact preservation. Data from these monitoring systems guide conservation decisions to maintain optimal conditions for the site.

Specialized conservation laboratories have been established to study and treat artifacts and inscriptions discovered within the catacombs. These laboratories use state-of-the-art equipment and materials to clean, restore, and preserve items, ensuring their longevity and protection from decay.

Virtual reality and augmented reality technologies allow visitors to experience the catacombs in a new way while minimizing physical impact. Virtual tours offer immersive experiences, providing insights into historical events and the significance of the catacombs' inscriptions.

Educational programs and workshops centered around the catacombs have been developed to engage the public, particularly young learners. By fostering an appreciation for cultural heritage and history, these initiatives create a new generation of advocates for preservation.

The historical significance of the Catacombs of Paris extends beyond national borders, attracting attention and interest from global preservation organizations. Collaborating with international partners facilitates knowledge exchange, funding opportunities, and expertise sharing, strengthening preservation efforts.

Given the catacombs' underground nature, emergency preparedness is vital. Regular drills and training exercises ensure that authorities and rescue teams are equipped to respond effectively to potential incidents within the catacombs.

Balancing tourism with preservation goals is a priority. Sustainable tourism initiatives focus on managing visitor numbers, creating responsible access points, and implementing environmentally friendly practices to minimize the impact of tourism on the catacombs.

Public engagement and advocacy efforts continue to be essential in promoting the preservation of the catacombs. Community support and public awareness campaigns foster a sense of ownership and responsibility for protecting this historical treasure.

The Catacombs of Paris stand as a living testament to history, preserving the memories and stories of millions of Parisians from centuries past. The collective efforts of experts, preservation organizations, authorities, and the public are crucial in safeguarding this enigmatic world beneath the bustling streets.

Through a combination of technological innovations, responsible tourism management, educational outreach, and international collaboration, the Catacombs of Paris continue to captivate and inspire visitors while remaining protected for future generations. The dedication to preserving this historical site ensures that the legacy of the catacombs will endure, allowing visitors to immerse themselves in the secrets of the past and appreciate the significance of this underground wonder for years to come.

EDWARD TURNER

Chapter 13: Beneath the Surface - Catacombs Art and Graffiti

―――

The Catacombs of Paris have become more than just an underground historical site; they have also become a canvas for a unique and secretive underground art scene. Deep within the forgotten chambers and secluded passages, a subculture of artists has found inspiration in the eerie and mysterious atmosphere of the catacombs.

1. Hidden Art Installations:

In the darkness of the catacombs, artists have created hidden art installations that surprise and delight those who stumble upon them. These art installations range from sculptures and paintings to elaborate light displays that transform the underground world into a surreal and captivating realm.

2. Graffiti and Street Art:

The catacombs' secluded corridors have attracted graffiti and street artists who use the dimly lit spaces as their canvas. The catacomb walls are adorned with colorful murals, tags, and intricate designs, blurring the lines between vandalism and artistic expression.

3. Photography and Filmmaking:

The haunting ambiance and otherworldly aesthetics of the catacombs have drawn photographers and filmmakers from around the world. Their work captures the enigmatic beauty of the underground realm, immortalizing its mystique in images and films.

4. Performance Art and Music:

Some artists have chosen the catacombs as a venue for performance art and music. Concerts, theatrical performances, and impromptu gatherings have taken place in the vast chambers, their haunting acoustics amplifying the emotional impact of these artistic expressions.

5. Spirit of Anonymity:

A unique aspect of the underground art scene in the catacombs is the spirit of anonymity. Many artists prefer to keep their identities hidden, allowing their work to speak for itself. This anonymity adds an air of mystery and intrigue to the art found within the catacombs.

6. Respect for the Space:

While the catacombs have become an underground art haven, the artists who venture into this world also respect the site's historical and cultural significance. Responsible artists aim to create art that enhances the catacombs' ambiance without causing damage or compromising its preservation.

7. Peril and Risk:

Creating art within the catacombs comes with its share of risks. Artists often venture into pitch-black tunnels, navigating challenging terrain and avoiding detection by authorities. This element of danger adds a sense of adventure and thrill to the underground art scene.

8. The Transience of Art:

In the catacombs, art is ever-changing and transient. As new artists discover the underground world, they leave their mark, replacing the old with the new. The catacombs thus become an ever-evolving gallery, reflecting the passage of time and the creativity of a diverse range of artists.

The Catacombs of Paris have become an underground art wonderland, where artists find inspiration in the haunting and hidden chambers. Through hidden installations, graffiti, photography, and performances, the catacombs transform into a unique and ever-changing art gallery.

The underground art scene within the catacombs pays homage to the site's rich history while challenging the boundaries of artistic expression. It remains an enigmatic subculture, thriving within the shadows, and adding a touch of artistic magic to the already mystical world of the Catacombs of Paris.

While the underground art scene within the catacombs adds an element of intrigue and creativity, it also raises ethical questions about the balance between artistic expression and the preservation of historical sites. Authorities responsible for the catacombs face the challenge of protecting the site's cultural heritage while acknowledging the allure of the art that has emerged within its depths.

Preservationists must carefully assess the impact of art installations on the catacombs' structural integrity and historical artifacts. Artwork that poses a risk to the site's preservation may need to be carefully removed or preserved through alternative means.

The underground art scene within the catacombs prompts a delicate balance between protecting the site's historical significance and allowing for artistic expression. Authorities and preservation organizations must carefully navigate the preservation of cultural heritage while respecting the creative spirit that has flourished in the catacombs.

For artists who wish to contribute to the underground art scene, respecting the catacombs' sanctity is essential. Art should be created with materials that do not harm the historical structures, and artists should avoid damaging or altering the catacombs' inscriptions and artifacts.

To maintain the transience and mystique of the underground art scene, artists can consider creating temporary and site-specific installations that do not leave a permanent mark on the catacombs. This approach allows for artistic expression while preserving the historical integrity of the site.

Dialogue between artists, preservationists, and authorities can foster understanding and mutual respect for both the historical and artistic aspects of the catacombs. Collaboration can lead to the development of guidelines that balance artistic freedom with responsible exploration.

SECRETS OF THE BONE LABYRINTH: THE HAUNTED CATACOMBS OF PARIS

Raising public awareness about the importance of preserving historical sites like the catacombs is crucial in promoting responsible artistic practices. Public education efforts can help artists and visitors understand the significance of the catacombs and the need for conservation.

The underground art scene within the Catacombs of Paris presents a fascinating juxtaposition of artistic expression and historical preservation. As the catacombs continue to be a canvas for creative minds, it is vital to strike a balance between the allure of artistic discovery and the importance of preserving cultural heritage.

Through collaboration, responsible practices, and public engagement, the catacombs can remain a living legacy where art and history coexist in a realm of enigmatic beauty. By honoring the historical significance of the site and respecting its sanctity, artists and preservationists alike contribute to the preservation of this underground wonderland for generations to come.

Graffiti artists are a diverse group of urban creatives who use public spaces, walls, and structures as their canvas for self-expression. Their works, known as graffiti or street art, often incorporate vibrant colors, intricate designs, and powerful messages that reflect the artist's identity, ideas, and emotions. The unique canvas they choose - the walls of cities and urban landscapes - sets graffiti art apart from more traditional forms of art and makes it an integral part of the contemporary urban culture.

Graffiti artists view the streets and city walls as an expansive and dynamic gallery. Unlike conventional art galleries, which may have strict rules and entry fees, the urban landscape offers a free and open space for artists to share their creations with a vast audience. This accessibility allows graffiti art to reach diverse communities, transcending socioeconomic barriers and bringing art directly to the people.

Many graffiti artists adopt pseudonyms or street names, allowing them to maintain anonymity while leaving their mark on the urban canvas. This anonymity offers a sense of freedom and protection, enabling artists to express themselves boldly without the constraints of public recognition or social judgment. Through their chosen pseudonyms, artists develop unique identities that become synonymous with their artistic style and message.

Graffiti art often serves as a form of social commentary and political protest. Artists use their works to address societal issues, challenge the status quo, and raise awareness about topics that matter to them. Graffiti can be a powerful medium for dissent and resistance, allowing artists to express dissenting opinions and provoke critical thinking.

Graffiti artists have a knack for transforming neglected and unremarkable spaces into visually engaging and thought-provoking environments. They breathe life into abandoned buildings, underpasses, and dull city walls, turning them into vibrant and dynamic spaces that captivate passersby.

SECRETS OF THE BONE LABYRINTH: THE HAUNTED CATACOMBS OF PARIS

Graffiti art has the unique ability to foster a sense of community and connection among artists and urban residents. It serves as a visual conversation, with different artists responding to one another's work, collaborating on projects, and contributing to the collective identity of a neighborhood or city.

The transient nature of graffiti art adds an element of impermanence and unpredictability to the urban landscape. Some works may stay for years, becoming part of the city's identity, while others may be painted over or removed quickly. This ephemeral quality adds an element of excitement to the discovery of new works and encourages artists to constantly reinvent their creative expression.

For many graffiti artists, their work is a form of activism. It allows them to reclaim public spaces, challenge the dominance of advertising and commercialization, and provide an alternative narrative to the consumer-driven urban environment.

Graffiti artists have carved a unique niche in the art world, transforming cityscapes into vibrant and expressive galleries. Their chosen canvas - the walls and structures of urban landscapes - offers a free and accessible platform for creative expression, social commentary, and community connection.

Graffiti art's ephemeral nature and anonymity contribute to its allure and controversy, sparking debates about the boundaries of art, public space, and individual expression. Whether celebrated as an authentic form of urban art or condemned as vandalism, graffiti artists continue to leave their mark on the cityscape, using their unique canvas to tell their stories and engage with the world around them.

Despite its undeniable creativity and impact, graffiti art faces several challenges and controversies:

1. Legal Issues:

Graffiti art often operates in a legal gray area, with many works considered vandalism and subject to legal repercussions. Artists risk fines, community service, or even imprisonment if caught creating unauthorized graffiti.

2. Property Rights and Consent:

The use of private property as a canvas without the owner's consent raises ethical questions about individual rights and property ownership. While some property owners welcome graffiti art, others view it as defacement and seek its removal.

3. Quality and Aesthetic:

Critics argue that not all graffiti qualifies as art, with some works being seen as mere tagging or visual pollution. The subjectivity of aesthetic appreciation often leads to debates over the artistic merit of specific pieces.

4. Cultural Appropriation and Respect:

Graffiti art occasionally faces criticism for cultural appropriation or insensitivity. Artists must be mindful of the cultures they reference and avoid using symbols or themes that may offend or perpetuate harmful stereotypes.

5. Environmental Impact:

Some graffiti materials, such as aerosol spray paint, can have negative environmental effects. Artists must consider using eco-friendly materials to reduce their environmental impact.

6. Gentrification and Commercialization:

As graffiti art gains popularity, it can be co-opted by corporations or used as a marketing tool, diluting its original intent and cultural significance. This commercialization can also lead to gentrification, displacing artists and erasing the unique character of urban neighborhoods.

7. Permanence and Preservation:

While the transient nature of graffiti is part of its charm, it also means that significant works may disappear over time. Preserving and documenting these art pieces for future generations can be challenging, especially when faced with the threat of removal or fading.

8. Negative Perception and Stigmatization:

Despite its growing acceptance as a legitimate form of art, graffiti still faces negative perception and stigmatization from some segments of society. This perception can hinder the integration of graffiti art into mainstream culture.

Graffiti art continues to evolve and challenge traditional notions of art and public space. While it faces controversies and legal challenges, its undeniable impact on urban culture and its ability to provoke thought and social commentary have secured its place as a dynamic and significant art form.

As public attitudes toward graffiti art evolve, there is a growing recognition of its potential to beautify urban spaces, promote community engagement, and create meaningful connections among city residents. Balancing artistic freedom with the need to respect public and private property remains an ongoing challenge, and constructive dialogue between artists, authorities, and the public is essential to find common ground and appreciate the unique canvas that graffiti art brings to the urban landscape.

Chapter 14: Reflections on the Haunted Catacombs

———

The enduring allure of the Catacombs of Paris lies in its captivating blend of history, mystery, and haunting beauty. This underground realm has become an integral part of Parisian culture, leaving an indelible mark on the city's identity and attracting millions of tourists each year. The Catacombs' impact on Parisian culture and tourism is multi-faceted, shaping the way locals and visitors perceive the city and connecting them with its rich historical past.

The Catacombs serve as a portal to Paris's past, offering a glimpse into the city's ancient history and the lives of its inhabitants. This connection to the past fosters a sense of historical continuity, reminding both Parisians and visitors that the city's present is built upon the legacy of its ancestors.

The enigmatic nature of the Catacombs has turned it into a symbol of mystery and intrigue. It embodies the idea that there are hidden secrets beneath the surface, waiting to be discovered. This allure extends beyond the catacombs themselves, influencing the perception of Paris as a city full of hidden stories and untold mysteries.

The Catacombs have become an integral part of Parisian cultural identity and heritage. They are a testament to the city's complex history, representing both moments of celebration and moments of tragedy. As a result, Parisians take pride in this unique aspect of their city and its rich cultural heritage.

The haunting allure of the Catacombs has inspired numerous artists, writers, and filmmakers over the years. Its dark and mysterious atmosphere serves as a backdrop for stories of suspense, horror, and adventure. As a result, the Catacombs have become a recurring motif in literature, art, and cinema, further cementing their significance in popular culture.

The Catacombs have become a major tourist attraction, drawing visitors from all over the world. Tourists are intrigued by the opportunity to explore this hidden underground world and witness the eerie spectacle of millions of bones arranged in intricate patterns. The Catacombs' popularity contributes significantly to Paris's tourism industry, attracting visitors and generating economic benefits for the city.

The Catacombs have also become a venue for cultural events and exhibitions. From art installations to historical exhibitions, the catacombs provide a unique setting for immersive experiences that further deepen the connection between visitors and the city's history.

Beyond the intrigue and spectacle, the Catacombs hold a deeper significance as a place of reflection and contemplation. Visitors are reminded of the transience of life and the universality of mortality, leading to moments of introspection and philosophical pondering.

The Catacombs of Paris stand as a mesmerizing testament to the city's past, a place where history, art, and mystery converge.

SECRETS OF THE BONE LABYRINTH: THE HAUNTED CATACOMBS OF PARIS

As an enduring symbol of Parisian culture, the Catacombs have left an indelible mark on the city's identity, shaping the way both locals and tourists perceive and connect with Paris.

The allure of the Catacombs extends beyond its dark corridors and skeletal displays; it embodies the eternal charm of hidden stories waiting to be unearthed. As long as its mysteries continue to captivate the imagination and draw curious souls from around the world, the Catacombs of Paris will remain an enduring symbol of the city's rich cultural heritage and an essential destination for those seeking to explore the enigmatic depths of history.

As the Catacombs of Paris continue to attract visitors from all corners of the globe, the responsibility of preserving this historical treasure becomes even more critical. Efforts to balance tourism with conservation are ongoing to ensure that future generations can also experience the allure of the Bone Labyrinth. Here are some measures being taken to preserve the legacy of the Catacombs:

1. Sustainable Tourism Management:

Authorities implement measures to manage tourism sustainably, limiting the number of visitors in designated sections and guiding tours to minimize the impact on the catacombs' fragile structures and artifacts.

2. Digital Preservation:

Advancements in technology allow for the digital preservation of the catacombs, creating 3D models and high-resolution images that document the site in its current state. This digital archive serves as a valuable resource for researchers and preservationists.

3. Conservation Initiatives:

Conservation efforts focus on repairing and maintaining the catacombs' structural integrity, as well as preserving the bones, inscriptions, and artworks found within. Restorations are conducted with great care to retain the authenticity and historical significance of the site.

4. Public Education and Awareness:

Public education initiatives aim to raise awareness about the historical importance of the Catacombs and the need to respect and preserve them. Informative exhibits and educational programs inform visitors about the catacombs' history, significance, and the impact of their actions on the site.

5. Collaborative Partnerships:

Collaboration with preservation organizations, researchers, and experts helps secure additional resources for the catacombs' conservation. By working together, stakeholders can pool their expertise and knowledge to protect this valuable historical site.

6. Responsible Tourism Promotion:

Efforts are made to promote responsible tourism, encouraging visitors to respect the catacombs' rules and regulations. Ethical tourism practices ensure that visitors appreciate the site's historical value without causing harm to the delicate underground environment.

7. Community Involvement:

Engaging the local community is essential in preserving the Catacombs of Paris. Residents take pride in their city's heritage and often participate in clean-up efforts and awareness campaigns to protect and maintain the catacombs.

8. Technological Monitoring:

Advanced monitoring technology tracks environmental conditions within the catacombs, enabling swift responses to potential threats like humidity, temperature changes, or structural instabilities.

The Catacombs of Paris stand as an enduring testament to the city's history, a timeless journey through the past that captivates hearts and minds alike. Its allure lies not only in its haunting beauty and enigmatic nature but also in the efforts made by authorities, preservationists, and the public to safeguard its cultural heritage.

As Paris continues to evolve and embrace modernity, the Catacombs remain a steadfast link to the city's past, a reminder of the lives that came before and the stories etched into the bone labyrinth. By preserving this unique underground wonder, Paris pays homage to its historical roots, allowing future generations to continue their voyage into the enigmatic world beneath the streets, forever enchanted by the enduring allure of the Catacombs of Paris.

The future of the Catacombs of Paris as an important historical and haunted landmark is likely to be shaped by a delicate balance between preservation, cultural appreciation, and responsible tourism management. As the Catacombs continue to capture the imagination of people worldwide, it is essential to consider several factors that will influence its trajectory in the years to come.

Preserving the Catacombs' structural integrity, inscriptions, and artifacts will remain a top priority. Continued efforts to monitor and assess the site's condition, implement restoration projects, and use modern preservation techniques will ensure that this historical landmark remains intact for future generations.

Cultural appreciation and education initiatives will play a vital role in shaping the Catacombs' future. Public awareness campaigns, educational programs, and interactive exhibits can deepen visitors' understanding of the site's historical and cultural significance. By fostering appreciation for the Catacombs' past, visitors will be more inclined to respect and protect this unique heritage.

Managing tourism responsibly will be essential to preserve the catacombs' haunted ambiance and historical value. Limiting the number of visitors, regulating tour groups, and implementing sustainable tourism practices will help minimize the impact on the site while offering visitors a meaningful and immersive experience.

SECRETS OF THE BONE LABYRINTH: THE HAUNTED CATACOMBS OF PARIS

Advancements in technology will continue to contribute to the Catacombs' future. Digital preservation, virtual reality tours, and interactive experiences will enable more people to access the catacombs' history and atmosphere while reducing physical strain on the site.

Collaboration among preservation organizations, historians, archaeologists, and paranormal researchers will enrich our understanding of the Catacombs' history and mysteries. Research and exploration efforts will shed light on untold stories, adding to the site's allure as a haunted landmark.

Support for the underground art scene within the Catacombs can coexist with preservation efforts. Encouraging responsible street art and cultural events can enhance the site's mystique and foster a sense of community among artists and visitors.

As a haunted landmark, the Catacombs will continue to intrigue those interested in the paranormal and ghostly legends. Urban legends and ghost stories will endure, adding an element of mystery to the site and attracting enthusiasts seeking supernatural experiences.

The Catacombs of Paris are destined to remain a timeless symbol of the city's past, an underground realm of history and haunting intrigue. With responsible preservation efforts, educational initiatives, and appreciation for its cultural significance, the Catacombs will continue to captivate the hearts and minds of locals and tourists alike.

By striking a careful balance between preservation and cultural appreciation, the Catacombs will endure as an essential historical and haunted landmark, guiding visitors on an immersive journey through Paris's past and offering a glimpse into the enigmatic and haunting depths of history. As it has for centuries, the Bone Labyrinth will remain an enduring and emblematic part of the City of Lights, shrouded in mystery and fascination for generations to come.

The Catacombs of Paris will continue to be an emblematic symbol of the city's history while embracing the modern era. As a historical landmark, it will remain a tangible link to the past, connecting present-day Parisians and visitors with the city's rich and multifaceted heritage.

Advancements in immersive technology will enhance the visitor experience within the Catacombs. Virtual reality tours and interactive exhibits will transport visitors back in time, allowing them to witness historical events and gain a deeper understanding of the catacombs' significance.

Continued research and archaeological discoveries may lead to the expansion of the catacombs' historical narratives. Previously unknown stories and aspects of life in Paris through the ages may come to light, enriching the site's allure and educational value.

Preservation efforts will be guided by sustainable practices, ensuring that future generations can also explore the Catacombs while preserving its haunting ambiance. New technologies and materials will be employed to protect the site's integrity while maintaining its authenticity.

SECRETS OF THE BONE LABYRINTH: THE HAUNTED CATACOMBS OF PARIS

The Catacombs will continue to host cultural events, exhibitions, and performances that celebrate Parisian culture and artistic expression. These events will weave the site's historical significance with modern creativity, breathing new life into its ancient chambers.

The Catacombs will remain a boundless source of inspiration for artists, writers, and filmmakers, inspiring countless works that perpetuate its legend and allure in popular culture.

The ghostly legends surrounding the Catacombs will persist, becoming an integral part of its identity as a haunted landmark. Ghost tours and paranormal investigations will allow visitors to delve into the eerie stories and embrace the mysteries of the underground world.

The Catacombs of Paris will serve as a symbol of the city's resilience and ability to preserve its history amid the evolving urban landscape. It will stand as a testament to the importance of protecting and appreciating historical landmarks that shape the collective identity of a city.

The Catacombs of Paris will continue to endure as an important historical and haunted landmark, captivating the imagination of all who venture into its depths. Its legacy will persist as a tangible link to Paris's past, a source of cultural appreciation, and a symbol of the city's ability to embrace both history and modernity.

The allure of the Catacombs lies not only in its chilling history but also in its timeless ability to evoke wonder and curiosity. As visitors traverse its ancient corridors and encounter the remains of millions of souls, they will be forever drawn to the haunting depths of the Bone Labyrinth, perpetuating its legacy as a timeless and enigmatic landmark in the heart of Paris.

SECRETS OF THE BONE LABYRINTH: THE HAUNTED CATACOMBS OF PARIS

Chapter 15: Catacombs Visitor Guide

―――

The Catacombs of Paris offer a unique and memorable experience, but visiting this historical site requires careful preparation and adherence to safety guidelines. Below is practical information and safety tips for those planning to explore the Catacombs:

1. Entry Requirements:

- The Catacombs are open to the public, but visitors must purchase tickets in advance. It is advisable to book tickets online to secure a specific entry time and avoid long queues.

- The Catacombs have restricted visitor capacity, so it's essential to plan your visit well in advance, especially during peak tourist seasons.

- Children under 14 years old are not allowed entry without an accompanying adult.

2. Access and Location:

- The official entrance to the Catacombs is located at 1 Avenue du Colonel Henri Rol-Tanguy, 75014 Paris, France.

- The site is easily accessible by public transportation. Take the Paris Metro and alight at the Denfert-Rochereau station (Lines 4 and 6) or the RER B line.

3. Dress Appropriately:

- The Catacombs have a consistent temperature of around 14°C (57°F), so it is advisable to wear comfortable clothing and sturdy shoes suitable for walking on uneven surfaces.

4. Safety Precautions:

- The Catacombs can be dark, narrow, and labyrinthine. Stay with your group and follow the designated paths to avoid getting lost.

- Be cautious of low ceilings and uneven floors to prevent tripping or hitting your head.

- Photography is generally allowed, but avoid using flash to maintain the solemn ambiance and prevent disturbing other visitors.

- Do not touch the walls or any artifacts. The catacombs are a protected historical site, and touching can cause damage or lead to accidents.

- There is no mobile phone signal in many parts of the Catacombs, so plan your visit accordingly and stay together with your group.

5. Respect the Sanctity of the Site:

- The Catacombs serve as the final resting place for millions of people. Show respect for the deceased and the historical significance of the site.

SECRETS OF THE BONE LABYRINTH: THE HAUNTED CATACOMBS OF PARIS

- Do not disturb the bones, inscriptions, or artwork within the Catacombs. Vandalism is strictly prohibited and can lead to legal consequences.

6. Consider a Guided Tour:

- To gain a deeper understanding of the Catacombs' history and significance, consider joining a guided tour led by experienced guides who can provide valuable insights and ensure safety.

7. Plan for Limited Facilities:

- There are limited restroom facilities within the Catacombs, so it is advisable to use the facilities before starting your visit.

- Carry water and any necessary snacks, as there are no food or drink vendors within the Catacombs.

8. Be Mindful of Your Health:

- The underground environment may not be suitable for those with claustrophobia, respiratory conditions, or mobility issues. Consult a doctor if you have any health concerns.

By following these practical tips and safety guidelines, visitors can make the most of their experience while respecting the solemnity and historical significance of the Catacombs of Paris. Enjoy your visit to this haunting and captivating underground world!

9. Stay Informed about COVID-19 Guidelines:

- Before your visit, check for any specific COVID-19 related guidelines and restrictions that may be in place for the Catacombs. Follow all health and safety protocols, including wearing masks and maintaining physical distancing.

10. Plan for Waiting Time:

- Even with advance tickets, there might be waiting time before entry. Be prepared for some waiting, especially during peak seasons, and plan your schedule accordingly.

11. Language Considerations:

- While English signage and information are available, consider carrying a translation app or guidebook if you are not fluent in French.

12. Check for Special Events and Closures:

- The Catacombs occasionally host special events or undergo maintenance, which might lead to partial or complete closures. Check the official website or contact the authorities in advance to ensure the site will be open during your planned visit.

13. Consider Your Emotional Sensitivity:

- The Catacombs can evoke strong emotions due to their historical significance and macabre nature. Consider your emotional sensitivity and preparedness for this experience.

14. Plan for Additional Exploration:

- The Catacombs represent just a fraction of the vast underground tunnel network beneath Paris. If you're interested in urban exploration, consider joining specialized tours to explore other parts of the underground city (cataphiles).

15. Support Preservation Efforts:

- By visiting the Catacombs responsibly and respecting the site's rules, you contribute to its preservation for future generations to enjoy.

16. Check for Nearby Attractions:

- The Catacombs are situated in a vibrant area of Paris. Consider exploring nearby attractions such as the Montparnasse Cemetery, Luxembourg Gardens, or the famous Montparnasse Tower for a complete experience.

17. Respect Local Regulations:

- Outside of the official entrance, access to other parts of the underground tunnel network is illegal and dangerous. Respect local regulations and do not attempt unauthorized exploration.

By adhering to these practical tips and safety guidelines, you can ensure a memorable and respectful visit to the Catacombs of Paris. The allure of this historical and haunted landmark will undoubtedly leave a lasting impression, as you embark on a journey through the eerie and enigmatic depths of the Bone Labyrinth beneath the City of Lights.

EDWARD TURNER

Chapter 16: The Catacombs in Popular Culture

─────

The Catacombs of Paris have captured the imagination of artists, writers, and filmmakers throughout history, inspiring a wide array of works across different mediums. From literature to films and art, the catacombs' haunting ambiance, historical significance, and enigmatic allure have left an indelible mark on popular culture. Let's explore how the catacombs have been depicted in various creative expressions:

1. Literature:

- Victor Hugo's "Les Misérables" (1862): In this iconic novel, the catacombs play a significant role in the plot. Jean Valjean, the protagonist, seeks refuge within the catacombs as he escapes from the authorities.

- Gaston Leroux's "The Phantom of the Opera" (1910): In this gothic tale, the catacombs serve as the mysterious lair of the Phantom, adding to the eerie atmosphere of the story.

- Edgar Allan Poe's "The Cask of Amontillado" (1846): Though not set in the Catacombs of Paris, Poe's classic short story features a dark and eerie underground setting reminiscent of the catacombs' ambiance.

2. Films:

- "As Above, So Below" (2014): This found-footage horror film follows a group of explorers who venture deep into the Catacombs of Paris, only to encounter supernatural and terrifying occurrences.

- "Catacombs" (2007): In this horror film, a young woman becomes lost in the Catacombs of Paris and must confront her fears as she navigates the dark and haunting tunnels.

- "Phantom of the Rue Morgue" (1954): In this classic horror film, a series of murders are linked to the Catacombs of Paris, adding a macabre element to the story.

3. Art:

- Théodore Géricault's "The Raft of the Medusa" (1819): This famous painting depicts the aftermath of the shipwreck of the French naval frigate Medusa. The artist visited the catacombs to study the bones and skeletons, which influenced his realistic depiction of the figures' emaciated bodies.

- Félix Vallotton's "Catacombs at Night" (1895): This painting captures the haunting atmosphere of the Catacombs of Paris, portraying the eerie tunnels and the remains of the deceased.

4. Photography:

- Nadar's Photographs (1860s): The renowned photographer Nadar captured some of the first images of the catacombs, documenting its haunting beauty and historical significance.

5. Music:

SECRETS OF THE BONE LABYRINTH: THE HAUNTED CATACOMBS OF PARIS

- "The Catacombs" by Steve Reich: This minimalist composition is inspired by the catacombs and creates a meditative and immersive musical experience.

6. Graphic Novels and Comics:

- "Catacombs" by Jung: This graphic novel explores the catacombs as a metaphorical journey into the subconscious mind of the protagonist.

7. Video Games:

- "Assassin's Creed Unity" (2014): This action-adventure video game features a virtual representation of the Catacombs of Paris, allowing players to explore its dark and intricate passages as they uncover historical secrets.

- "The Council" (2018): This narrative-driven adventure game includes the catacombs as one of its mysterious and atmospheric locations, where players must navigate treacherous tunnels to uncover hidden truths.

8. Theatre:

- "Catacombs" by Marc Frost: This play explores the catacombs as a setting for a gripping and atmospheric tale, delving into the themes of life, death, and the human psyche.

9. Documentaries:

- "The Catacombs of Paris" (Various): Several documentaries have been made to explore the history, significance, and mysteries of the Catacombs of Paris, shedding light on their role in shaping the city's past.

10. Fashion and Photography Shoots:

- The catacombs' unique aesthetic and haunting ambiance have attracted photographers and fashion designers, who have used the underground world as a striking backdrop for photoshoots and artistic projects.

11. Web Series and Online Media:

- With the rise of online content, various web series and online media have featured the Catacombs of Paris, discussing its history, legends, and urban exploration adventures.

12. Literary Adaptations:

- Numerous adaptations of classic literature that feature the catacombs as a setting or source of inspiration have been created for the stage and screen, reimagining these timeless stories with a catacomb backdrop.

The Catacombs of Paris have proven to be a timeless and enduring source of inspiration for artists across diverse forms of creative expression. Their dark, mysterious, and haunting allure continues to captivate the collective imagination, making them a rich and versatile canvas for storytelling, art, and exploration.

From classic literary works to contemporary video games and virtual experiences, the catacombs have left an indelible mark on popular culture, becoming a symbol of history, intrigue, and the enigmatic world beneath the streets of Paris. As long as the catacombs continue to hold their allure and allure, they will remain a compelling and enduring subject in the world of literature, films, art, and beyond.

The Catacombs of Paris have had a profound influence on the horror genre and popular culture, serving as a captivating and chilling setting for various works of fiction, films, and other forms of entertainment. Here are some ways the catacombs have impacted the horror genre and popular culture:

1. Haunting Ambiance:

The catacombs' dark and claustrophobic tunnels, lined with neatly arranged skulls and bones, create an atmosphere of eerie and macabre beauty. This haunting ambiance has been used as a setting for numerous horror stories, providing a perfect backdrop for tales of suspense, mystery, and supernatural encounters.

2. Mysterious and Enigmatic Lore:

The catacombs' rich history and legends of ghostly apparitions and curses have fueled the imagination of writers, filmmakers, and artists. These enigmatic stories have become a staple of horror narratives, adding layers of mystery and intrigue to the catacombs' portrayal in popular culture.

3. Exploration and Adventure:

The underground maze-like structure of the catacombs lends itself to stories of exploration and adventure, often involving characters navigating the dark tunnels while facing various challenges and dangers. The catacombs' complex layout provides an ideal setting for thrilling pursuits and escapes.

4. Supernatural Encounters:

The catacombs' association with death and the macabre makes it a natural location for supernatural encounters and ghostly apparitions. Many horror stories set in the catacombs feature restless spirits, vengeful ghosts, and other supernatural entities, heightening the fear factor and adding to the overall sense of dread.

5. Themes of Mortality and Decay:

The catacombs' walls adorned with skulls and bones serve as a visual reminder of mortality and the inevitability of death. These themes are often woven into horror narratives, exploring the human psyche and our fear of the unknown and the afterlife.

6. Urban Legends and Ghost Stories:

The Catacombs of Paris have inspired numerous urban legends and ghost stories that have been passed down through generations. These tales of cursed visitors, ghostly processions, and phantom guardians have become part of popular folklore, contributing to the catacombs' reputation as a haunted and mysterious place.

7. Influence on Film and Television:

The catacombs have been a recurring location in horror films and television shows. From psychological thrillers to supernatural horror, filmmakers have utilized the catacombs' haunting setting to create suspenseful and terrifying scenes.

8. Dark Tourism and Urban Exploration:

The Catacombs of Paris have become a significant destination for dark tourism and urban exploration. Thrill-seekers and adventurers are drawn to the catacombs' allure, seeking an adrenaline rush as they explore the hidden world beneath the city streets.

9. Influence on Art and Photography:

The catacombs' haunting beauty has inspired artists and photographers to capture its surreal and otherworldly essence. Various art forms, from paintings to installations, have incorporated the catacombs as a subject, evoking its eerie and captivating nature.

The Catacombs of Paris have left an indelible mark on the horror genre and popular culture. Their haunting ambiance, rich history, and enigmatic lore have made them a recurring and enduring source of inspiration for creators and storytellers alike. As long as the catacombs continue to hold their air of mystery and fascination, they will remain a staple in the world of horror and a cherished icon of popular culture.

10. Symbolism of Death and Transformation:

The Catacombs of Paris represent a powerful symbol of death and transformation, making them a potent thematic element in horror narratives. Writers and filmmakers often use the catacombs as a metaphor for the darker aspects of human existence, exploring themes of mortality, decay, and the passage of time. The juxtaposition of the catacombs' somber bones with the vibrancy of life above ground serves as a stark reminder of the impermanence of life.

11. Cultural Impact and Tourism:

The influence of the Catacombs of Paris extends beyond the horror genre and seeps into broader popular culture. Tourists from around the world visit the catacombs, seeking an experience that connects them with history, mystery, and the supernatural. The catacombs' popularity as a tourist attraction demonstrates their enduring allure as an iconic symbol of Paris and its rich cultural heritage.

12. Exploration of Human Psyche:

Horror narratives set in the catacombs often delve into the human psyche, exploring fear, anxiety, and the primal instinct for survival. The confined spaces, darkness, and historical association with death create an ideal backdrop for stories that delve into the depths of human emotions and primal fears.

13. Expansion of Subgenres:

The catacombs' influence has extended to various subgenres of horror, such as found-footage horror, psychological horror, and paranormal thrillers. From found-footage films that simulate the experience of urban exploration to psychological horror stories that play on fear and uncertainty, the catacombs have provided fertile ground for diverse horror narratives.

14. Reinventing the Haunted Setting:

SECRETS OF THE BONE LABYRINTH: THE HAUNTED CATACOMBS OF PARIS

The catacombs have offered a fresh and unique haunted setting that differs from traditional haunted houses or abandoned buildings. Their historical significance and status as an actual burial site add a layer of authenticity and gravity to horror stories set within their depths.

15. Preservation and Public Awareness:

The portrayal of the Catacombs of Paris in horror and popular culture has helped raise public awareness about their historical significance and the need for their preservation. The interest generated by these works has contributed to increased efforts to safeguard the catacombs as an essential heritage site.

16. Influence on Haunted Attraction and Theme Parks:

The haunting allure of the Catacombs of Paris has found its way into haunted attractions and theme parks around the world. Attractions inspired by the catacombs replicate their eerie atmosphere, providing visitors with a taste of the macabre and supernatural.

17. Thematic Inspiration for Other Horror Settings:

The catacombs' haunting and mysterious ambiance has inspired the creation of similar settings in horror narratives. Underground catacombs, ossuaries, and burial sites have become recurring elements in horror fiction, thanks to the enduring influence of the Catacombs of Paris.

The Catacombs of Paris have had a profound and lasting impact on the horror genre and popular culture. Their haunting allure, enigmatic history, and symbolic significance have made them a sought-after setting for horror narratives, exploring themes of mortality, fear, and the supernatural. As a result, the catacombs have become an enduring icon of horror and a captivating destination for those seeking an unforgettable experience of dark allure and historical mystique.

The Catacombs of Paris have had a profound influence on the horror genre and popular culture, serving as a captivating and chilling setting for various works of fiction, films, and other forms of entertainment.

The catacombs' dark and claustrophobic tunnels, lined with neatly arranged skulls and bones, create an atmosphere of eerie and macabre beauty. This haunting ambiance has been used as a setting for numerous horror stories, providing a perfect backdrop for tales of suspense, mystery, and supernatural encounters.

The catacombs' rich history and legends of ghostly apparitions and curses have fueled the imagination of writers, filmmakers, and artists. These enigmatic stories have become a staple of horror narratives, adding layers of mystery and intrigue to the catacombs' portrayal in popular culture.

The underground maze-like structure of the catacombs lends itself to stories of exploration and adventure, often involving characters navigating the dark tunnels while facing various challenges and dangers. The catacombs' complex layout provides an ideal setting for thrilling pursuits and escapes.

The catacombs' association with death and the macabre makes it a natural location for supernatural encounters and ghostly apparitions. Many horror stories set in the catacombs feature restless spirits, vengeful ghosts, and other supernatural entities, heightening the fear factor and adding to the overall sense of dread.

The catacombs' walls adorned with skulls and bones serve as a visual reminder of mortality and the inevitability of death. These themes are often woven into horror narratives, exploring the human psyche and our fear of the unknown and the afterlife.

The Catacombs of Paris have inspired numerous urban legends and ghost stories that have been passed down through generations. These tales of cursed visitors, ghostly processions, and phantom guardians have become part of popular folklore, contributing to the catacombs' reputation as a haunted and mysterious place.

The catacombs have been a recurring location in horror films and television shows. From psychological thrillers to supernatural horror, filmmakers have utilized the catacombs' haunting setting to create suspenseful and terrifying scenes.

The Catacombs of Paris have become a significant destination for dark tourism and urban exploration. Thrill-seekers and adventurers are drawn to the catacombs' allure, seeking an adrenaline rush as they explore the hidden world beneath the city streets.

The catacombs' haunting beauty has inspired artists and photographers to capture its surreal and otherworldly essence. Various art forms, from paintings to installations, have incorporated the catacombs as a subject, evoking its eerie and captivating nature.

The Catacombs of Paris represent a powerful symbol of death and transformation, making them a potent thematic element in horror narratives. Writers and filmmakers often use the catacombs as a metaphor for the darker aspects of human existence, exploring themes of mortality, decay, and the passage of time. The juxtaposition of the catacombs' somber bones with the vibrancy of life above ground serves as a stark reminder of the impermanence of life.

The influence of the Catacombs of Paris extends beyond the horror genre and seeps into broader popular culture. Tourists from around the world visit the catacombs, seeking an experience that connects them with history, mystery, and the supernatural. The catacombs' popularity as a tourist attraction demonstrates their enduring allure as an iconic symbol of Paris and its rich cultural heritage.

Horror narratives set in the catacombs often delve into the human psyche, exploring fear, anxiety, and the primal instinct for survival. The confined spaces, darkness, and historical association with death create an ideal backdrop for stories that delve into the depths of human emotions and primal fears.

The catacombs' influence has extended to various subgenres of horror, such as found-footage horror, psychological horror, and paranormal thrillers. From found-footage films that simulate the experience of urban exploration to psychological horror stories that play on fear and uncertainty, the catacombs have provided fertile ground for diverse horror narratives.

The catacombs have offered a fresh and unique haunted setting that differs from traditional haunted houses or abandoned buildings. Their historical significance and status as an actual burial site add a layer of authenticity and gravity to horror stories set within their depths.

The catacombs have been a recurring location in horror films and television shows. From psychological thrillers to supernatural horror, filmmakers have utilized the catacombs' haunting setting to create suspenseful and terrifying scenes.

The Catacombs of Paris have become a significant destination for dark tourism and urban exploration. Thrill-seekers and adventurers are drawn to the catacombs' allure, seeking an adrenaline rush as they explore the hidden world beneath the city streets.

The catacombs' haunting beauty has inspired artists and photographers to capture its surreal and otherworldly essence. Various art forms, from paintings to installations, have incorporated the catacombs as a subject, evoking its eerie and captivating nature.

The portrayal of the Catacombs of Paris in horror and popular culture has helped raise public awareness about their historical significance and the need for their preservation. The interest generated by these works has contributed to increased efforts to safeguard the catacombs as an essential heritage site.

The haunting allure of the Catacombs of Paris has found its way into haunted attractions and theme parks around the world. Attractions inspired by the catacombs replicate their eerie atmosphere, providing visitors with a taste of the macabre and supernatural.

The catacombs' haunting and mysterious ambiance has inspired the creation of similar settings in horror narratives. Underground catacombs, ossuaries, and burial sites have become recurring elements in horror fiction, thanks to the enduring influence of the Catacombs of Paris.

The Catacombs of Paris have had a profound and lasting impact on the horror genre and popular culture. Their haunting allure, enigmatic history, and symbolic significance have made them a sought-after setting for horror narratives, exploring themes of mortality, fear, and the supernatural. As a result, the catacombs have become an enduring icon of horror and a captivating destination for those seeking an unforgettable experience of dark allure and historical mystique.

SECRETS OF THE BONE LABYRINTH: THE HAUNTED CATACOMBS OF PARIS

Chapter 17: A Never-Ending Enigma

As visitors descend into the dark and labyrinthine depths of the Haunted Catacombs of Paris, they embark on a journey that transcends time, history, and mortality. The haunting allure of this underground world, lined with millions of bones, holds a profound fascination that has captivated the human imagination for centuries. It is a place where the past and the present converge, where the boundary between the living and the dead blurs, and where the whispers of long-forgotten souls echo through the shadows.

The Catacombs of Paris stand as a testament to the fragility of human existence and the enduring allure of the unknown. They have served as an inspiration for tales of horror and mystery, as well as a canvas for artists seeking to capture the eerie beauty of mortality. These subterranean passageways continue to be a symbol of the human fascination with life and death, with history and the supernatural.

Amidst the bone-lined walls and winding corridors, one can't help but feel a sense of reverence and humility. The catacombs remind us of the transient nature of life, the impermanence of all things, and the unending passage of time. They beckon us to contemplate our own mortality and the mysteries that lie beyond the veil of the known.

As we emerge from the depths of the Bone Labyrinth and return to the bustling streets of Paris, the enigma of the Haunted Catacombs remains. Their allure endures, an ever-present reminder that even in the most ordinary places, there may be hidden worlds filled with stories of the past and echoes of the spirits that once wandered these ancient halls.

The Haunted Catacombs of Paris continue to intrigue and mesmerize, inviting us to explore the shadows of the human psyche and the mysteries that lie beneath the surface. In their haunting beauty, they are a reminder of the fragility of life, the resilience of memory, and the enduring fascination with the unknown. As long as these ancient tunnels lie beneath the streets of Paris, they will continue to beckon adventurers, artists, and dreamers, offering a glimpse into a realm where history, legend, and imagination intertwine, and the allure of the mysterious and haunted remains eternal.

In the realm of the Haunted Catacombs of Paris, the past remains ever-present, casting its spectral veil over the living. The legends and ghostly tales woven into the catacombs' very fabric infuse the air with an undeniable sense of mystery and intrigue. It is a place where the ordinary transforms into the extraordinary, where history's secrets linger like elusive phantoms, just beyond our grasp.

As we ponder the enigmatic markings etched into the walls, the hidden messages that have withstood the test of time, we realize that the Catacombs of Paris are more than a mere burial site. They are a time capsule of stories, emotions, and lives long gone but never truly forgotten.

SECRETS OF THE BONE LABYRINTH: THE HAUNTED CATACOMBS OF PARIS

The allure of the catacombs is not merely confined to dark tourism or urban exploration; it extends beyond the confines of physical space. It resides in the collective consciousness of humanity, forever haunting our imaginations and sparking our curiosity.

In the catacombs' enduring mystery, we find a mirror of our own mortality. We are reminded that, like the bones that line the tunnels, we too shall one day return to the earth, leaving behind our own stories and legacies. The catacombs become a reminder that life is fleeting, but the echoes of our existence can endure through the ages.

In this hidden realm beneath the City of Light, we are beckoned to confront the fears that lurk in the dark corners of our minds, to explore the depths of human emotion, and to embrace the unknown with a mix of trepidation and wonder. The Catacombs of Paris teach us that even in the most haunting of places, beauty can be found – a beauty that transcends the macabre and offers a poignant reminder of the cyclical nature of life and death.

So, as the echoes of history reverberate through the underground chambers, let us marvel at the enduring mystery and fascination surrounding the Haunted Catacombs of Paris. For within their depths, a timeless allure awaits – an allure that compels us to contemplate our place in the vast tapestry of existence and to embrace the ephemeral beauty that life offers.

Sign up to my free newsletter to get updates on new releases, FREE teaser chapters to upcoming releases and FREE digital short stories.

Or visit https://tinyurl.com/olanc

I never spam and you can unsubscribe at any time.

Don't miss out!

Visit the website below and you can sign up to receive emails whenever Edward Turner publishes a new book. There's no charge and no obligation.

https://books2read.com/r/B-A-SYIZ-ZQMMC

BOOKS 2 READ

Connecting independent readers to independent writers.

Also by Edward Turner

The Kraken Quest: Exploring the Mythical Giants of the Sea
Secrets of the Bone Labyrinth: The Haunted Catacombs of
Paris

About the Author

Edward Turner is a renowned author who specializes in exploring the realms of ghosts, the paranormal, and cryptids. With a captivating writing style and an insatiable curiosity for the unknown, Turner has garnered a dedicated following of readers who are captivated by his thrilling and eerie tales.

Born with an innate fascination for the supernatural, Turner has spent decades delving into the depths of paranormal phenomena, unearthing captivating stories and untangling mysteries that lie beyond the veil of the ordinary. His extensive research and meticulous attention to detail have earned him a reputation as a leading authority in the field.

Through his books, Turner expertly weaves together chilling accounts of encounters with ghosts, offering readers a glimpse into the ethereal world that coexists alongside our own. His ability to paint vivid portraits of spectral apparitions and convey the haunting atmosphere of haunted locations has made his works both spine-tingling and thought-provoking.

Turner's exploration of the paranormal doesn't stop at ghosts. He also dives into the fascinating world of cryptids—creatures that defy conventional explanation. His in-depth investigations into legendary creatures such as Bigfoot, the Loch Ness Monster, and the Chupacabra showcase his commitment to shedding light on these enigmatic beings.

With each page, Edward Turner's readers are drawn deeper into the enigmatic and unknown. His unique storytelling ability combined with his meticulous research has made him a sought-after author for those with an insatiable thirst for the supernatural. Whether delving into ghostly encounters or unraveling the mysteries of elusive cryptids, Turner's books offer a spine-chilling and immersive reading experience that leaves readers questioning the boundaries of our reality.

Edward Turner's works have earned critical acclaim and numerous accolades within the paranormal genre. He continues to explore the unexplained, captivating readers with his distinctive narrative style and unwavering dedication to unveiling the mysteries that lie hidden in the shadows.